STRATEGIES
FOR TEACHING
Strings and Orchestra

MENC wishes to thank
Carolynn A. Lindeman for developing and coordinating this series;
Dorothy A. Straub, Louis S. Bergonzi, and *Anne C. Witt*
for selecting, writing, and editing the strategies for this book;
and the following teachers for submitting strategies:

Michael M. Alexander	Priscilla M. Howard	Mel Pontious
Michael A. Allard	Robert H. Klotman	Sally Pullen
Nathan M. Artley	Ed Krebs	Mark Ribbens
Gilles Bonneau	Susan Krebs	Janine H. Riveire
Karin Boyce	Jerrell Lambert	Marion Roberts
Andrew H. Dabczynski	Jerrie Lucktenberg	Debbie Rohwer
Edwin C. de Groat	Teresa J. McCreary	Margaret Schmidt
Jacquelyn Dillon-Krass	Loretta J. W. McNulty	Darwyn Snyder
Susan P. Ellington	Tamara Mason	Adrienne Thompson
Joanne Erwin	Carrie Miller	Benjamin Whitcomb
Doris Gazda	John Moon	Janice Williams
Robert S. Genualdi	Judy Palac	Michele Winter
Brian L. Hartle	Andrew Perea	Gary Wolfman

YOUR KEY TO
IMPLEMENTING
THE NATIONAL
STANDARDS
FOR MUSIC
EDUCATION

STRATEGIES FOR TEACHING

Strings and Orchestra

MENC

MUSIC EDUCATORS NATIONAL CONFERENCE

COMPILED
AND EDITED
BY
Dorothy A. Straub,
Louis S. Bergonzi,
and
Anne C. Witt

CONTENTS

PREFACE

The Music Educators National Conference (MENC) created the *Strategies for Teaching* series to help preservice and in-service music educators implement the K–12 National Standards for Music Education and the MENC Prekindergarten Standards. To address the many components of the school music curriculum, each book in the series focuses on a specific curricular area and a particular level. The result is eleven books spanning the K–12 areas of band, chorus, general music, strings/orchestra, guitar, keyboard, and specialized ensembles. A prekindergarten book and a guide for college music methods classes complete the series.

The purpose of the series is to seize the opportunity presented by the landmark education legislation of 1994. With the passage of the Goals 2000: Educate America Act, the arts were established for the first time in our country's history as a core, challenging subject in which all students need to demonstrate competence. Voluntary academic standards were called for in all nine of the identified core subjects—standards specifying what students need to know and be able to do when they exit grades 4, 8, and 12.

In music, content and achievement standards were drafted by an MENC task force. They were examined and commented on by music teachers across the country, and the task force reviewed their comments and refined the standards. While all students in grades K–8 are expected to meet the achievement standards specified for those levels, two levels of achievement—proficient and advanced—are designated for students in grades 9–12. Students who elect music courses for one to two years beyond grade 8 are expected to perform at the proficient level. Students who elect music courses for three to four years beyond grade 8 are expected to perform at the advanced level.

The music standards, together with the dance, theatre, and visual arts standards, were presented in final form—*National Standards for Arts Education*—to the U.S. Secretary of Education in March 1994. Recognizing the importance of early childhood education, MENC went beyond the K–12 standards and established content and achievement standards for the prekindergarten level as well, which are included in MENC's *The School Music Program: A New Vision*.

Now the challenge at hand is to implement the standards at the state and local levels. Implementation may require schools to expand the resources necessary to achieve the standards as specified in MENC's *Opportunity-to-Learn Standards for Music Instruction: Grades PreK–12.* Teachers will need to examine their curricula to determine if they lead to achievement of the standards. For many, the standards reflect exactly what has always been included in the school music curriculum—they represent best practice. For others, the standards may call for some curricular expansion.

To assist in the implementation process, this series offers teaching strategies illustrating how the music standards can be put into action in the music classroom. The strategies themselves do not suggest a curriculum. That, of course, is the responsibility of school districts and individual teachers. The strategies, however, are designed to help in curriculum development, lesson planning, and assessment of music learning.

The teaching strategies are based on the content and achievement standards specified in the *National Standards for Arts Education* (K–12) and *The School Music Program: A New Vision* (PreK–12). Although the strategies, like the standards, are designed primarily for four-year-olds, fourth graders, eighth graders, and high school seniors, many may be developmentally appropriate for students in other grades. Each strategy, a lesson appropriate for a portion of a class session or a complete class session, includes an objective (a clear statement of what the student will be able to do), a list of necessary materials, a description of what prior student learning and experiences are expected, a set of procedures, and the indicators of success. A follow-up section identifies ways learning may be expanded.

The *Guide for Music Methods Classes* contains strategies appropriate for preservice instructional settings in choral, instrumental, and general music methods classes. The teaching strategies in this guide relate to the other books in the series and reflect a variety of teaching/learning styles.

Bringing a series of thirteen books from vision to reality in a little over a year's time required tremendous commitment from many, many music educators—not to mention the tireless help of the MENC publications staff. Literally hundreds of music teachers across the country answered the call to participate in this project, the largest such participation in an MENC publishing endeavor. The contributions of these teachers and the books' editors are proudly presented in the various publications.

—*Carolynn A. Lindeman*
Series Editor

Carolynn A. Lindeman, professor of music at San Francisco State University, served on the MENC task force that developed the music education standards. She is the author of three college textbooks (The Musical Classroom, PianoLab, and MusicLab) and numerous articles.

INTRODUCTION

The National Music Standards and School String and Orchestra Programs: Understanding the Variations

The National Standards for Music Education may be the dominant theme in school music education for the remainder of the century. This publication demonstrates how these voluntary national music standards relate to one aspect of contemporary school string and orchestra education, namely the instructional process.

The teaching strategies in this volume are designed for string and orchestra classes in grades 5 through 12 and organized around the nine music content standards found in the *National Standards for Arts Education*, published by MENC. These strategies are an important step in transforming the standards from being simply a professional document to being an influence on student learning. They represent the work of string and orchestra educators and are guidelines for teaching within the framework set forth by the new music standards.

It is important to consider how the music standards relate to the structure of orchestra programs (i.e., lessons, orchestras, and small ensembles) and how individual teachers might begin to derive their own teaching strategies from the standards. As stated in the music standards and in MENC's opportunity-to-learn standards, (1) not all music departments offer the opportunity for students to learn stringed instruments, and (2) there are many instructional paths to the same goal. Thus, the process of applying the music standards to string and orchestra programs must include the identification of certain variations of the theme.

Variations in Applying the Music Standards to String and Orchestra Programs

School string and orchestra programs do not exist unto themselves. They are part of an overall school music program that provides students with an education in music, and that program, in turn, is a part of the total educational package offered by a school district. In most cases the string and orchestra program is an elective proposition augmenting the classroom music sequence. The string or orchestra program is not the sole provider of a comprehensive music education, and the music standards do not suggest it be so.

The music standards, therefore, are to be applied to each component of the music program, but not with equal emphasis.[1] For although many orchestra teachers have their students sing in their classes, that does not mean that they are attempting to address Content Standard 1: "Singing, alone and with others, a varied repertoire of music." It should be fairly obvious that this music standard is best achieved in the classroom music or choral setting.[2] Therefore, the number of teaching strategies included here for each of the standards varies.

Variations in Opportunities to Learn

The music standards define what all students should know and be able to do. Not all students, however, attend schools that support music instruction to the same degree—especially to the extent of offering strings. Only 35 percent of American elementary schools offer students the opportunity to study stringed instruments, 19 percent of large American middle schools have symphonic orchestras and 45 percent offer string orchestra,[3] and 31 percent of American high schools offer orchestra or string classes.[4]

Clearly this situation represents the most dramatic obstacle to students' opportunities to learn stringed instruments; for students can't learn to play them if they are not offered in their schools. How can anyone expect that all students will meet the same music standards given the enormous variation in school district and music department course offerings—or, simply put, given an unequal opportunity to learn?

In response to this reality, MENC has developed a set of visionary opportunity-to-learn standards for music, which are enumerated in the *Opportunity-to-Learn Standards for Music Instruction,* published by MENC. Whereas the national music standards define what all students should know and be able to do in music, the opportunity-to-learn standards describe the context for student learning—that is, the school music program.

The opportunity-to-learn standards define standards for curriculum and scheduling, staffing, materials and equipment, and facilities. With regard to string curriculum and scheduling, they call for instruction on stringed instruments to begin not later than grade 4, with beginning instruction available in upper grades as well. Given the limited number of string and orchestra programs in schools, an enormous amount of work needs to be done to ensure that all American schools offer students the opportunity to study strings.

Creating Your Own Variations from the Sample Teaching Strategies

The teaching strategies in this collection are examples of the contributors' plans of how they would teach so that over time they could bring their students toward a particular achievement standard. Each strategy is a part of a lesson-planning process and does not necessarily represent the final demonstration of an exit standard for a particular grade.

The school string and orchestra teachers who wrote these strategies have shared ideas about teaching strings that work in their circumstances. Thus, these teaching strategies in their current form do not apply to all situations. The strategies should be modified to suit a particular teacher's situation, much as recipes from a cookbook are altered to suit individual tastes, health concerns, kitchen resources, and cooking skills. Examine the sample strategies and consider how they might work for you and your students, keeping in mind their essential relationship to the voluntary national music standards.

Assumptions

The teaching strategies in this publication are presented under the following assumptions:

1. Teachers can provide some type of aural-visual model of string performance.

    Many of the teaching strategies, particularly those for students younger than high school, include teacher modeling as an instructional technique. Modeling is important because words are but representations of musical sound and because words do not show students what good string technique looks like. Although this reliance on musical models may reflect the influence of Suzuki pedagogy on contemporary string teaching, the use of modeling in teaching music is centuries old.

The simplest way to provide a model is by teacher demonstration; however, not all teachers who teach strings may be able to do this.[5] Teachers with limited string skills should consider modifications to a strategy that requires a model, such as asking more advanced players to demonstrate. Another possibility is to provide alternative musical models by singing or chanting or using electronic musical media (i.e., recordings, music technology). Teachers may also offer visual models without an instrument by demonstrating the physical gestures of string playing.

2. Typically, orchestra teachers spend more instructional time teaching string students than those who study other instruments; for wind and percussion students, instruction is largely the responsibility of the band teacher. Although many of the strategies in this collection are intended for string classes and string orchestras, teachers may easily apply or adapt them for use with symphony orchestras.

3. String students have the opportunity to study and perform solo and chamber music literature as part of their experience in a school string and orchestra program. A complete string program includes solo and small-ensemble experiences, which are important vehicles for achieving the music standards.

Things to Keep in Mind

While reading through the strategies, keep in mind the following points:

1. Instruments are not listed under the heading Materials; it is assumed that the students are prepared with their instruments and that you, the teacher, have your instrument.

2. Specific arrangements and their publishers are not listed unless the teaching strategy requires a particular published version of a piece.

3. When a strategy calls for the students to play a piece for a particular purpose, such as determining the form or meter, one should assume that the students are proficient enough on their instruments to do so.

4. Although all strategies are tied to both a content and an achievement standard, in some cases a strategy may not address all aspects of the particular achievement standard. This is because the strategies were developed to be implemented during a single class meeting.

Notes

1. At the school district level, the most obvious manifestation is that, as the introduction to *The School Music Program: A New Vision* states, the music standards are intended for all students through grade 8, but for only those students who enroll in music from grades 9 through 12 (p. 2).

2. Strategies involving singing are included in this collection, however.

3. Charles Leonhard, *Status of Arts Education in American Public Schools* (Urbana, IL: National Arts Education Research Center, University of Illinois at Urbana–Champaign, 1991). A large middle school is one with five hundred or more students.

4. Louis S. Bergonzi, "The National Standards in Music Education: A Call for Comprehensive Music Education for All Children," in *Loyola University Music Education Leadership Symposia: Implications of National Music Standards for String Education,* ed. Gwen Hotchkiss (Elkhardt, IN: United Musical Instruments, 1995).

5. The non–string player who has the responsibility for teaching strings should try to acquire some degree of string-playing skill. These professional skills contribute to student achievement as well as teacher satisfaction.

STRATEGIES
Grades 5–8

STANDARD 1C

Singing, alone or with others, a varied repertoire of music: Students sing music representing diverse genres and cultures, with expression appropriate for the work being performed.

Objective

- Students will sing and play a selection with appropriate phrasing, dynamics, and musical expression.

Materials

- "Song of Jupiter" by George Frideric Handel, arr. Leroy Anderson (Boca Raton, FL: Edwin F. Kalmus & Company, 1952), Level 3
- Copies of vocal music for "Where'er You Walk," from *Semele* by Handel
- Piano

Other Requirements

- Tenor (perhaps a faculty member, a parent, a local church musician, or a mature high school student) prepared to sing "Where'er You Walk" in the key of G major at an artistic level
- Piano accompanist

Prior Knowledge and Experiences

- In either string or full orchestra, students can play "Song of Jupiter" with accurate pitch and rhythm at an appropriate tempo.
- Students have had experience singing melodic lines in their orchestra music.

Procedures

1. Explain to students that the piece they have been learning, "Song of Jupiter," is an orchestral arrangement of the song "Where'er You Walk," which is from *Semele* by Handel.
2. Ask tenor soloist to sing "Where'er You Walk" with piano accompaniment. Have students listen carefully to the phrasing and musical expression of the melodic line, particularly as it relates to the text of the song.
3. Have students play "Song of Jupiter" as the soloist repeats the song. Ask them to reflect the style, phrasing, and expression of the soloist in their playing.
4. Ask students to describe various aspects of the music, such as legato style, expressive melodic lines, phrasing, dynamics, and balance of melody and accompaniment.
5. Distribute copies of "Where'er You Walk" and ask students to sing the melody with the soloist and piano accompaniment. Ask students to focus on the aspects of the music that they have discussed.
6. Conduct orchestra in performing the entire "Song of Jupiter" once again, this time without the soloist. Ask students to perform the music as artistically as possible, based on their listening, discussion, and singing experience.
7. Ask students to evaluate their performance by commenting particularly on the style, phrasing, dynamics, balance, and overall expression. If appropriate, ask soloist to comment on students' performance and to give suggestions.

Indicators of Success

- Students sing "Where'er You Walk" and play "Song of Jupiter" with appropriate phrasing, dynamics, and musical expression.

Follow-up

- Have students follow a similar procedure with other orchestral selections based on songs (for example, "Greensleeves").

Performing on instruments, alone and with others, a varied repertoire of music: Students perform on at least one instrument accurately and independently, alone and in small and large ensembles, with good posture, good playing position, and good breath, bow, or stick control.

Objective

- Students will identify aurally in-tune and out-of-tune strings and tune them on their own stringed instruments accurately and independently.

Materials

- Electronic tuner
- Fine tuners for all strings on all instruments

Prior Knowledge and Experiences

- Students have participated in a beginning string class for at least two months.

Procedures

1. Tell the class that they are going to tune their own instruments. Say, "Listen to the A," and have the electronic tuner briefly sound A 440.

2. Take a student's instrument and adjust the A string fine tuner so that the string goes extremely flat.

3. Have the student play the out-of-tune string while the electronic tuner again sounds A 440 so that the class can compare the two pitches. Ask the class to raise their hands first if they think the string is too high in relation to the tuner and then if they think the string is too low. Discuss their responses with them and help them decide who is right.

4. Demonstrate the process for adjusting the fine tuners: "right to tight," "left to loose." Have the class repeat the rhyme several times. Explain that if the string is too low, it will need to be tightened; if it is too high, it will need to be loosened. Have the student adjust the fine tuner based on the class's determination of what needs to be done. Help the class determine whether their decision was correct, having the student readjust the fine tuner if necessary.

5. Have each student adjust the A string fine tuner on his or her instrument after listening to A 440 on the electronic tuner.

Indicators of Success

- Students identify out-of-tune strings and adjust them using the fine tuners.

Follow-up

- In subsequent classes, continue the ear-training and tuning practice. Class could show how the fine tuner on the A string needs to be adjusted (in comparison to the A 440 of the electronic tuner) on a classmate's instrument by pointing down for lower, up for higher, and level for exactly in tune.

Performing on instruments, alone and with others, a varied repertoire of music: Students perform on at least one instrument accurately and independently, alone and in small and large ensembles, with good posture, good playing position, and good breath, bow, or stick control.

Objective

- Students will demonstrate correct right-hand playing position, including bow hold, finger placement, and direction of moving bow.

Materials

- Cakes of rosin

Prior Knowledge and Experiences

- Students have mastered the basic left-hand playing position.
- Students have developed the ability to play first-position notes of a major tetrachord on at least two strings pizzicato.
- Students can read simple open-string notes and rhythms in the method book.

Procedures

1. Make three marks on your hand and on each student's bow hand with a pen: an "X" on the side of the first finger between the first and second joint; a dot on the tip of the thumb; and a line on the middle finger at the crease on the second joint. For cellos and basses, the line extends across the middle, third, and pinky fingers along the second joint crease.

2. Take a pencil and hold it so that the marks on your hand touch the pencil.

3. Replace the pencil with the bow. Assist each student in establishing a good bow hold with check points of dot, line, and X. (*Note:* Each bow has a balance point somewhere between the frog and the tip. Starting at the balance point is recommended to prevent tension.) When the student is comfortable holding the bow at the balance point and getting a good sound, have the student gradually move the right hand to the frog, still referring to check points for contact.

4. Lead students in bow games, moving the bow in the air while keeping the fingers placed correctly on the bow.

5. Demonstrate and ask students to imitate the following: Hold the rosin in the left hand as if it were an instrument. Take the bow in the right hand, holding it correctly at the frog, and place it on the rosin with the right hand on top of the left hand. Pull the bow to the right, away from the rosin, and say "down-bow." Reverse the

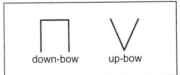

motion and say "up-bow." Ask students to notice that the symbol for down-bow is the shape of the frog of the bow and the symbol for up-bow is the shape of the tip of the bow. Have students say "down-bow" and "up-bow" as they move their bows in the proper direction. (This not only teaches the two directions but conditions the bows for playing since many may be new and in need of a heavy application of rosin.)

(continued)

Indicators of Success

- Students duplicate correct right-hand playing position, as illustrated in most method books.

- Holding the bow correctly, students draw a down-bow and an up-bow.

Follow-up

- At each subsequent class, check all aspects of the bow hold, making adjustments as needed, with attention to moving the bow perpendicular to the string, using the weight of the arm to increase the pressure on the string in order to produce a solid sound.

Performing on instruments, alone and with others, a varied repertoire of music: Students perform on
at least one instrument accurately and independently, alone and in small and large ensembles, with
good posture, good playing position, and good breath, bow, or stick control.

Objective

- Students will play with a full, resonant sound on their instruments.

Materials

- None required

Prior Knowledge and Experiences

- Students have developed good left-hand and right-hand playing positions.

Procedures

1. Have students practice turning an imaginary doorknob counter clockwise using their right hand, wrist, and forearm, and then release it slowly to spring back clockwise. Students should keep hand on "doorknob" to provide resistance while it springs back.

2. In playing position, have students quietly set the middle of the bow on a selected string.

3. Have students pronate their right forearm (turn the doorknob) counter clockwise, causing the bow stick to bend. Check to assure that students keep the bow hair flat on the string. The bow should be perpendicular to the string. Have students release the pressure with a clockwise motion.

4. Have students repeat steps 2 and 3. Direct students to drop (relax) the right elbow, then pull the bow to the tip. When students get to the tip of the bow, have them push the bow to the frog.

5. Have students move the bow from the frog to the tip using the counter clockwise motion and from the tip to the frog using the clockwise motion.

6. Repeat steps 1–5 until students can draw a beautiful tone.

Indicators of Success

- Students produce a full, resonant sound.

Follow-up

- Have students apply this technique to produce a full, rich sound on a simple piece of music.
- Have students apply this technique, rotating the hand, in playing shorter strokes at the frog, the middle, and the tip of the bow.

Performing on instruments, alone and with others, a varied repertoire of music: Students perform on at least one instrument accurately and independently, alone and in small and large ensembles, with good posture, good playing position, and good breath, bow, or stick control.

Objective

- Students will identify major and minor scale patterns and through imitation will play the patterns on all four strings.

Materials

- None required

Prior Knowledge and Experiences

- Students are able to hold the instruments correctly and play pizzicato and arco on all open strings.

Procedures

1. To establish major and minor scale patterns, demonstrate the following finger games while students imitate. Hold up your left hand with palm facing you and with fingers extended. Explain left-hand finger patterns.

    a. *For violin and viola:* (1) Spread the hand so that there is space between all fingers except between first and second fingers, which are touching. Identify this as a minor scale pattern (1-2 3 4). (2) Change the pattern so that there is space between all fingers except second and third fingers, which are touching. Identify this as a major scale pattern (1 2-3 4).

    b. *For cello:* (1) Identify open 1 2 as a minor scale pattern. (2) Identify open 1 3 as a major scale pattern.

    c. *For bass:* (1) Identify open 1 2 as a minor scale pattern. (2) Identify open 1 4 as a major scale pattern.

2. With students having instruments in playing position, demonstrate while students imitate.

    a. *For violin and viola:* Place fingers on the fingerboard in the minor pattern, then slide the second finger to change to the major. Right hand may be used to support the instrument.

    b. *For cello:* Practice open 1 2 finger placement, then open 1 3 finger placement.

    c. *For bass:* Practice open 1 2 finger placement, then open 1 4 finger placement.

3. Now, with students playing the instruments, demonstrate, then have students imitate, the following sequences on one string:

violin/viola:	0000	1111	2222 (minor)	1111	0000	1111	2222 (major)	1111	0000
cello:	0000	1111	2222 (minor)	1111	0000	1111	3333 (major)	1111	0000
bass:	0000	1111	2222 (minor)	1111	0000	1111	4444 (major)	1111	0000

4. Ask students to repeat the sequence on each of the other three strings.

5. Lead students through the same sequence, reducing the repetitions to three, then two, and then one.

6. Demonstrate, then have students imitate, sliding (violin and viola)/alternating (cello and bass) the following fingering patterns:

violin/viola:	00	11	22 (minor)	22 (major)	22 (minor)	22 (major)	22 (minor)	11	00
cello:	00	11	22 (minor)	33 (major)	22 (minor)	33 (major)	22 (minor)	11	00
bass:	00	11	22 (minor)	44 (major)	22 (minor)	44 (major)	22 (minor)	11	00

7. Demonstrate, then have students imitate, "Hot Cross Buns" (pizzicato or arco), using the major scale pattern; then have them change to the minor scale pattern and play the piece in a minor key.

Indicators of Success

- Students identify and play the major and minor scale patterns on all strings.

Follow-up

- Demonstrate, then have students imitate, "Mary Had a Little Lamb" (three-note version) using the major scale pattern. Change to the minor scale pattern and play the piece in a minor key.

- Teach students to use major and minor scale patterns in other melodies, such as "Frère Jacques."

Performing on instruments, alone and with others, a varied repertoire of music: Students perform on at least one instrument accurately and independently, alone and in small and large ensembles, with good posture, good playing position, and good breath, bow, or stick control.

Objective

- Students will identify written and aural examples of an octave, explain what an octave is, and perform an octave with accurate intonation.

Materials

- Any string method book that introduces octaves
- Numerous written examples of octaves

Prior Knowledge and Experiences

- Students can perform a major tetrachord on each string accurately with correct hand position and can perform scales beginning on an open string.

Procedures

1. Examine words that relate to numbers, starting with familiar examples (a triangle, the Pentagon in Washington, D.C., and a quartet). Have students think of examples of various words that start with the prefix "oct," such as octagon (eight sides, like a stop sign), octopus (a sea animal with eight legs), octavo-size paper (paper that is eight inches long), octet (eight people singing or playing together), and octuplets (eight animals born together). Establish from the examples that the prefix "oct" means eight. In music, it means eight notes apart (the first part of the definition of an octave).

2. Have the class count the number of notes performed as you play the D major scale starting on the open D string. Ask the class to identify the letter name of the eighth note, the final note of the scale. (Third finger on the A string for violins and violas and fourth finger for cello; fourth finger in third position on the G string for bass.) The answer "D" will show the second part of the definition of an octave: two pitches with the same pitch name.

3. Explain to the class that if the fingered D is in the correct place, it will sound "nice," or consonant, when played with the open string below. Have students practice playing the two strings at once, sounding the octave. To do so, ask them to find the octave by sliding the finger for the fingered D while playing both strings, then adjusting and holding the correct pitch.

4. Have students find and play other octaves formed by playing an open string and a fingered string: G and A for the violin, C for the viola and cello, and A and E for the bass.

5. Ask students to identify octaves in a line of music. Then ask them to perform the line of music containing the octave and adjust the octave for accurate intonation. Have students identify and play additional lines of music containing octaves.

Indicators of Success

- Students explain that an octave is two pitches of the same name that are eight notes apart.
- Students name, play, and adjust the intonation of octaves played with an open string and a fingered string.
- Students identify octaves and play simple pieces that contain octaves.

Follow-up

- Find passages in orchestra music where two or more instruments are playing in octaves. Have these instruments play together and tune the octaves.
- As students become more advanced, point out other finger patterns for playing octaves—e.g., on violin and viola, 1 and 4 on adjacent strings; on cello, 3 (low note) and 1 (high note), using the first and third strings or second and fourth strings; on bass, 1 (low note) and 4 (high note), using the first and third strings or second and fourth strings.

Performing on instruments, alone and with others, a varied repertoire of music: Students perform on at least one instrument accurately and independently, alone and in small and large ensembles, with good posture, good playing position, and good breath, bow, or stick control.

Objective

- Students will perform a simple tune using open strings and third fingers (violin/viola) or fourth fingers (cello/bass) with accurate intonation, correct rhythm, accurate bowing, and a steady pulse.

Materials

- "Sweet-Eyed Sue," in *New Tunes for Strings,* Book 1, by Stanley Fletcher, instructional design by Paul Rolland (New York: Boosey & Hawkes, 1971)
- Piano

Prior Knowledge and Experiences

- Students have established finger placement for octaves and perfect fourths.

Procedures

1. Review matching octave patterns on two adjacent strings with resonant sound resulting from sympathetic vibrations (violin/viola, open to 3; cello/bass, open to 4).

2. Have students recite the rhythm pattern of the song "Sweet-Eyed Sue," using the counting system that is routinely used.

3. Without instruments, have students recite finger numbers as they tap the particular finger on the left thumb in rhythm, lifting all fingers for open strings (for example, 3 3 open).

4. Have students prepare to play pizzicato by checking the pitch of the fingered note with the open string an octave below. Then have students play the entire tune pizzicato.

5. Have students perform the tune with bows. Then add the piano accompaniment. If necessary, shadow bow the rhythm first, having students follow their parts and perform the bowing silently in the air.

Indicators of Success

- Students perform with accurate intonation, rhythm, and bowing, with and without accompaniment. When accompaniment is added, students maintain melody independently.

- Students maintain correct left-hand position.

Follow-up

- Use the same steps in approaching new music: first without the instrument, then pizzicato, and finally with the bow, checking consistently for accurate intonation and correct left-hand position.

Performing on instruments, alone and with others, a varied repertoire of music: Students perform on at least one instrument accurately and independently, alone and in small and large ensembles, with good posture, good playing position, and good breath, bow, or stick control.

Objective

■ Students will perform a given scale as a round, gaining experience in playing a part that is independent of other sections of the orchestra.

Materials

■ None required

Prior Knowledge and Experiences

■ Students are able to perform the D major scale with ease.

■ Students have had unison playing experience but only limited experience in playing a part that is independent of the other sections of the orchestra.

Procedures

1. Ask students to perform a D major scale in unison in quarter notes in 4/4 meter—four notes per pitch, ascending and descending, without repeating the top note.

2. Divide the group in half to perform the scale, instructing the second half of the group to wait for a cue to begin. When the first half begins the third degree of the scale, cue the second half to begin on the first note of the scale.

3. Ask students to play the scale as a round again, this time with only two quarter notes per pitch. Have the second half of the orchestra begin the round this time.

4. Ask students to repeat the round with only one quarter note per pitch.

Indicators of Success

■ Students successfully perform a scale as a round.

Follow-up

■ Further subdivide the orchestra by sections (first and second violins; violas; cellos and basses), by gender, by stand, or by individual and perform the scale as a three-part round, as a four-part round, and so on. Change the order of entrances frequently.

■ Use different rhythms for the scale.

■ Use the playing of scales as rounds as a warm-up for orchestras at all levels.

Performing on instruments, alone and with others, a varied repertoire of music: Students perform on at least one instrument accurately and independently, alone and in small and large ensembles, with good posture, good playing position, and good breath, bow, or stick control.

Objective

- Students will use dynamic contrast to perform melody and harmony parts in balance.

Materials

- A class ensemble book, such as *Primo Performance* by Robert S. Frost (San Diego: Neil A. Kjos Music Company, 1994), with a melody and a harmony part for every instrument

Prior Knowledge and Experiences

- Students have learned a two-part piece with easily distinguishable melody and harmony lines.

Procedures

1. Have all students play the melody first and then the harmony of the two-part piece they have been rehearsing.

2. Divide the ensemble into two groups with one playing the melody and the other the harmony. Ask students to listen to and describe how these two parts complement each other.

3. Have students perform and listen to different "balance" combinations of melody and harmony. First, have five students volunteer to play the melody and one student volunteer to play the harmony. Then reverse, having five students play the harmony and one play the melody.

4. Discuss the two versions with the students, asking whether either one was balanced.

5. Ask students whether it would be possible for the out-of-balance combinations in step 3 to become balanced. Ask them who would have to play louder or softer. Have volunteers demonstrate. Discuss how good balance can be achieved in any piece of music.

6. Have all students play the piece through (half playing the melody and half playing the harmony), observing proper balance.

Indicators of Success

- Students demonstrate their understanding of the difference between melody and harmony through playing and discussion.

- Students apply their listening skills in performance by modifying balance through dynamic contrast.

Follow-up

- Have students learn "Little Waltz in G" by Franz Schubert, arr. C. Paul Herfurth, in *Early Classics for Beginning String Quartet or String Orchestra* (Boston: Boston Music Company, 1965). Point out that the viola has the most important part, the cello and bass have the countermelody, and the violins have the accompanying figure. Work for a balanced performance.

- Have students draw or paint a simple picture (of a family or a sailboat, for example). Have half the class create pictures that are balanced (with the focal point centered, relatively equal space around it, and other objects in proportion to the focal point); have the other half of the class create pictures that are not balanced. Share the results with the class and discuss the effects on the viewer. Compare this perception to musical performance that is balanced versus unbalanced.

STANDARD 2B

Performing on instruments, alone and with others, a varied repertoire of music: Students perform with expression and technical accuracy on at least one string, wind, percussion, or classroom instrument a repertoire of instrumental literature with a level of difficulty of 2, on a scale of 1 to 6.

Objective

- As they perform an instrumental work with a level of difficulty of 2, students will control their bows and play with an even, sustained tone from the frog to the tip (down-bow) and return (up-bow) without diminishing the intensity of the sound in the upper half of the bow.

Materials

- "Intrada," from *Suite for Strings* by Samuel Scheidt, arr. Robert Klotman (Van Nuys, CA: Alfred Publishing Company, 1982), Level 2

Prior Knowledge and Experiences

- Students have had some experience with bowing exercises that use all parts of the bow.
- Students are able to play scales in C major, F major, B-flat major, G major, and D major.

Procedures

1. After explaining that this lesson will focus on developing a sustained, even sound using the whole bow, demonstrate a C major scale with three beats for each bow stroke ($\quarternote$=60) without applying weight in the upper half of the bow. Allow the sound to diminish naturally as the bow approaches the tip.

2. Ask students to listen to the sound or tone as it seems to diminish with a decrescendo effect. Have them identify the place in the bow stroke where the sound begins to diminish.

3. Demonstrate a reversed bow hold with the tip of the bow being held in the hand and the frog serving as the tip. Ask students to hold the bow in this manner.

4. Demonstrate the C major scale with this inverted position of the bow and ask students to note that as the bow is being drawn, there is an added weight, especially from the middle of the bow to the tip (which is now the frog), which helps maintain the intensity of the sound. Ask students to imitate the use of the bow in this manner.

5. With the bow now held properly at the frog, ask students to play the *meno mosso* section (from measure 48 to the end of "Intrada").

6. Ask students to reverse the bow, holding it at the tip, and play the same eight-measure excerpt. Have them note the improvement in a sustained sound.

7. Have students perform the complete "Intrada," holding the bow properly at the frog and maintaining the same sensation and intensity of sound that they experienced with the reversed bow hold.

Indicators of Success

- Students increase weight on the bow moving from the middle to the tip, thus improving intensity of the tone throughout the performance of the composition.

Follow-up

- Have students apply this technique to similar passages in other music, producing a rich, sustained sound. Choose a slow legato-style piece, such as "Air for Strings" by Norman Dello Joio (Miami: Belwin Mills/Warner Bros. Publications, 1967), Level 3, or "Andante Festivo" by Jean Sibelius (New York: Southern Music Company, 1941), Level 3. Focus on sustaining and "singing" the melodic lines by using full bow strokes with an intense sound and smooth bow changes.

Performing on instruments, alone and with others, a varied repertoire of music: Students perform with expression and technical accuracy on at least one string, wind, percussion, or classroom instrument a repertoire of instrumental literature with a level of difficulty of 2, on a scale of 1 to 6.

Objective

- Students will understand and use a systematic approach to learning a new instrumental work with a level of difficulty of 2.

Materials

- "Lightly Row," in *Suzuki Violin School*, vol. 1, by Shinichi Suzuki (Secaucus, NJ: Summy-Birchard, 1978), with letter names above the notes

- Finger chart of "Lightly Row" with rhythm symbols above the numbers

Prior Knowledge and Experiences

- Students are able to hold the bow and instrument in the correct playing position and can produce both good pizzicato and bowed tones.

- Students understand the importance of correct finger placement for pitch accuracy.

- Students are able to play the five rhythmic variations devised by Suzuki on the D major scale and "Twinkle, Twinkle Little Star" (in unison).

Procedures

1. Play "Lightly Row" for the students and have them *watch* the finger chart and music and *listen*. Tell students that to learn any new piece, they should learn the rhythm first, the pitches second, and technical demands third, and, finally, they should identify skills and knowledge they have learned in previous works. When all four of these steps are completed, they will memorize the piece, pluck it, and play it using the bow.

2. Have students say the rhythm using rhythmic syllables as you perform the piece again. Then have students say the rhythm without your playing the piece.

3. Have students sing or say the pitches (finger numbers or letters) in rhythm as you perform it. Repeat small sections until they have memorized the entire piece.

4. Tell students that the new technique in "Lightly Row" is stopping one string while playing another. Have students show the correct fingering for F-sharp on the D string. Tell students that while fingering F-sharp, they must be able to produce a good open A sound; in order to do that, they must have correct position. Demonstrate a good open A sound, with the string continuing to vibrate after it is plucked, and demonstrate the "thump" (the sound of a string when it is not free to ring); tell students that the finger must not touch the open string. Have students identify the good sound and the thump. Then have them demonstrate their understanding by fingering F-sharp on the D string and producing a resonant open A string sound at the same time.

5. Have students find the segments of the D major scale in "Lightly Row" (D E F# G A; D E F#; E F# G), and have them recognize that this is part of a previously learned skill.

6. Have students pluck the entire piece from memory. Tell them to remember to have F-sharp down before they begin the piece and to leave it down during the "triad place" (D F# A).

7. Lead students in playing the song arco, having them strive for long sustained tones with the bow never stopping. Repeat this step, adding dynamics.

Indicators of Success

- Students identify the steps that are part of this systematic approach to learning a new piece of music—isolating rhythmic, pitch, and technical aspects; identifying previously learned skills and techniques; memorizing the work; plucking it; and bowing it.

Follow-up

- Introduce a new piece (for example, "May Song," in *Suzuki Violin School,* vol. 1. Follow the same systematic steps.

- Introduce a new piece (for example, "Long, Long Ago," in *Suzuki Violin School,* vol. 1) and ask students to follow the same systematic steps independently and individually. Challenge the students to learn a new piece on their own and play it for the class.

STANDARD 2C

Performing on instruments, alone and with others, a varied repertoire of music: Students perform music representing diverse genres and cultures, with expression appropriate for the work being performed.

Objective

- Students will identify and play articulations and bowings of the Classical style in a work with a level of difficulty of 2.

Materials

- "Classical Dance" by Ken Cooper (Phoenix, AZ: C. R. Reiter Publishing, 1992), Level 2, or another piece in the Classical style in which articulations and bowings are not marked

Prior Knowledge and Experiences

- Students can play "Classical Bash," in *Strictly Strings,* Book 2, by Jacquelyn Dillon, James Kjelland, and John O'Reilly (Van Nuys, CA: Alfred Publishing Company, 1993), Level 1, with correct articulations and bowings, or another piece in the Classical style in which articulations and bowings are marked.

Procedures

1. Have the orchestra perform the first melodic motive (measures 1–8) in "Classical Dance."
2. Ask students which notes need more emphasis and which beats of the measure need more emphasis to make their playing more expressive.
3. Demonstrate the various bowings used for upbeats to a measure: up-down, down-up, or up-up.
4. Ask each section of the orchestra to discuss the bowing possibilities (including slurs), to make a decision as to the most appropriate bowing, to demonstrate that bowing for the class, and to provide a rationale for their decision.
5. Have students play the entire piece using the bowing each section has chosen.

Indicators of Success

- Students identify articulation and appropriate bowings for up-beats and weak and strong beats, as well as slurring techniques to accommodate strong beats throughout "Classical Dance."
- Students develop their own interpretation of style and articulation for playing music of the Classical period.

Follow-up

- Choose a Classical piece that includes markings for bowings and articulations. Ask students in each section whether they agree or disagree with the bowings and articulations.
- Choose a Classical piece or musical excerpt that does not include bowings or articulations. Ask students in each section to determine bowings and articulations appropriate to the Classical style.

STANDARD 2D

Performing on instruments, alone and with others, a varied repertoire of music:
Students play by ear simple melodies on a melodic instrument and simple
accompaniments on a harmonic instrument.

Objective

■ Students will echo a four-beat motif on their instruments.

Materials

■ None required

Prior Knowledge and Experiences

■ Students are able to hold instruments correctly, to produce a musical sound on their instruments, and to play the open strings and at least one finger on each string.

■ Students know the names of the notes they can play.

Procedures

1. Ask students to echo the notes and rhythm that you play.

2. Identify the starting note; play a four-beat motif and have students echo it.

3. Repeat the motif with students echoing several times until all students are successful.

4. Ask a student to identify the ending note.

Indicators of Success

■ Students echo back the correct pattern of pitches in rhythm.

Follow-up

■ Have students echo increasingly complex motifs appropriate to their level. For variety, use a combination of singing and playing.

■ Have students lead the echo game.

STANDARD 2D

Performing on instruments, alone and with others, a varied repertoire of music:
Students play by ear simple melodies on a melodic instrument and simple
accompaniments on a harmonic instrument.

Objective

- Students will imitate and create melodic patterns culminating in a complete song.

Materials

- Any simple melody (for example, "Happy Birthday" or "Frère Jacques")

Prior Knowledge and Experiences

- Students have some experience in imitating simple melodic patterns.

Procedures

1. Play the entire simple melody. Then play short, simple, stepwise patterns found in the melody to be learned, and ask students to echo the patterns. Do the same with patterns that include skips.

2. Model small sections of the melody, asking students to echo, until the melody is complete.

3. Play the entire melody and ask individual students to echo.

4. Ask the ensemble to play the entire melody.

5. Ask for a volunteer to play the melody while all other students play along silently.

Indicators of Success

- By ear, students perform basic patterns with movement by steps and skips. They combine basic patterns into longer melodic settings.

- Students perform complete rote-learned songs.

Follow-up

- Continue to use this methodology on a regular basis using longer and more complex tunes as the students become more skillful. This works well with a twelve-bar blues progression; for example, "Happy Blues," in *All for Strings,* Book 1, by Gerald E. Anderson and Robert S. Frost (San Diego, CA: Neil A. Kjos Music Company, 1982).

Performing on instruments, alone and with others, a varied repertoire of music: Students perform with expression and technical accuracy a varied repertoire of instrumental literature with a level of difficulty of 3, on a scale of 1 to 6, including some solos performed from memory.

Objective

- Students will develop ease in shifting from first to third to fifth positions and know the names of the notes in positions on all four strings, resulting in the ability to perform orchestral and solo literature at a more advanced level (3 on a scale of 1 to 6).

Materials

- Handouts (or diagrams on chalkboard) of rote fingering drill (see step 1) and of Shifting Drills 1, 2, and 3 (see steps 3, 4, and 5)

- Handouts of Fingerboard Worksheet for Shifting Drill 3 (see accompanying figure)

  [*Note:* Shifting Drills and Worksheet by Susan P. Ellington. Used by permission.]

Prior Knowledge and Experiences

- Students have established correct playing position, are able to play a tetrachord on each string and have some experience shifting into third position.

Procedures

1. Have students begin playing the basic drill—two notes per pitch on the G string. Instruct the students to continue repetitions on the G string until they hear the word "change," at which time they will change to the D string and continue the pattern, then "change" to the A string, then to the C/E strings.

2. After establishing the basic drill, have students play the scale with one note per pitch. Manually assist those who need help.

3. Lead students through Shifting Drill 1 on each string, which takes them to third position.

   SHIFTING DRILL 1

   ```
                 I          III      I
   VLN/VLA:  0  1  2  -  1  1  -  2  1  0
                        V      III  V    I
                 I          III      I
   CELLO:    0  1  3  -  1  1  -  3  1  0
                        V      III  V    I
                 I          III      I
   BASS:     0  1  4  -  1  1  -  4  1  0
                        V          V
   ```

4. Lead students through Shifting Drill 2 on each string, which takes them to third position plus a whole step (a major tetrachord).

   SHIFTING DRILL 2

   ```
                 I          III          I
   VLN/VLA:  0  1  2  -  1  2  2  1  -  2  1  0
                        V      III          V
                 I          III          I
   CELLO:    0  1  3  -  1  3  3  1  -  3  1  0
                        V      III          V
                 I          III          I
   BASS:     0  1  4  -  1  4  4  1  -  4  1  0
                        V                  V
   ```

5. Lead students through Shifting Drill 3 on each string, which takes them from first to third and then to fifth position with a major scale pattern all on one string (see example). Ask students to say the letter names as they play in order to reinforce learning the names of the notes in the position.

   SHIFTING DRILL 3

   ```
                 I          III      V                III      I
   VLN/VLA:  0  1  2  -  1  2  -  1  2  3  3  2  1  -  2  1  -  2  1  0
                        V      III  V      V    V          III  V    I
                 I          III      V                III      I
   CELLO:    0  1  3  -  1  3  -  1  3  3  3  3  1  -  3  1  -  3  1  0
                        V      III  V      V    V          III  V    I
                 I          III      V                III      I
   BASS:     0  1  4  -  1  4  -  1  4  3  3  4  1  -  4  1  -  4  1  0
                        V                V      V              V
   ```

(continued)

Indicators of Success

- Students play a major scale pattern with acceptable intonation on each string using the Shifting Drill 3 finger pattern.
- Students label Fingerboard Worksheet for Shifting Drill 3 (see figure) with note names, position number, and fingering on all strings for their instrument.

Follow-up

- Extend the drill by adding various bowings.

- Apply this shifting technique to specific scale passages in music being performed in class.

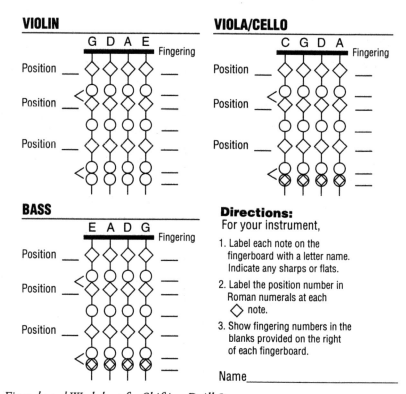

Fingerboard Worksheet for Shifting Drill 3.

STANDARD 2E

Performing on instruments, alone and with others, a varied repertoire of music: Students perform with expression and technical accuracy a varied repertoire of instrumental literature with a level of difficulty of 3, on a scale of 1 to 6, including some solos performed from memory.

Objective

■ Students will shift with ease and accuracy throughout the range of their instruments, resulting in the ability to perform orchestral and solo literature at a more advanced level (3 on a scale of 1 to 6).

Materials

■ *Rosamunde Overture* by Franz Schubert, arr. Vernon Leidig (Van Nuys, CA: Highland-Etling/Alfred Publishing Company, 1991), Level 3

Prior Knowledge and Experiences

■ Students have established correct left-hand position and have played Schubert's *Rosamunde Overture* in first position (wherever possible).

Procedures

1. To prepare for shifting, demonstrate and ask students to imitate a silent exercise. Slide each finger along one string, maintaining contact with the string without depressing it to the fingerboard (minimizing friction). Ask students to notice the space between the string and fingerboard. (*Note:* Omit basses when shifting with third finger.)

2. Establish a rhythm pattern (a dotted half note slurred to a quarter note at a slow tempo) for the exercises that follow.

In steps 3–6, demonstrate the exercise first; then have students imitate.

3. Begin with shifts on a single finger from first to third position. Play first-position note (B with the first finger on the A string) for two beats. On beat three, begin slow, pianissimo shift with the first finger by reducing finger and bow pressure, slowing bow speed, and leading with the wrist to avoid tension. On beat four, arrive at the target pitch in the third position (D with the first finger), listening for the approach to the pitch to avoid overshooting it.

4. Repeat third-position note (D), holding it for two beats; on beat three, prepare for descending shift by moving thumb and wrist back toward first position; release finger and bow pressure to achieve a pianissimo shift of the first finger down to the note B. Prepare and shift during beat three, arriving on beat four. Note to students that they should look at fingertip to see that there is space between the string and fingerboard during shift.

5. Using the above exercise, shift from first to third position on each finger and repeat the exercise on each string.

6. For violins and violas: Using the same exercise, still at a slow tempo, shift from first-position note (which will serve as tonic of its key) to each step of its major scale. It is advisable at first to shift only from first finger to second finger and back, first finger to third finger and back, first finger to fourth finger and back, and so on.

7. Lead the orchestra in playing *Rosamunde Overture,* asking students to shift at specific places in each part.

(continued)

Indicators of Success

- Students shift accurately and confidently from first position to higher positions when performing the *Rosamunde Overture*.

Follow-up

- Identify and have students practice passages from solo literature that can involve shifting on one finger to the same finger and then from one finger to a different finger (e.g., on violin, Handel sonatas).

- Have students apply refined shifting technique to increasingly more advanced orchestral literature—for example, Symphony no. 1, Fourth Movement, by Johannes Brahms, arr. Vernon Leidig (Van Nuys, CA: Highland-Etling/Alfred Publishing Company, 1990), Level 3, or the first movement of Schubert's "Unfinished" Symphony.

STANDARD 3A

Improvising melodies, variations, and accompaniments:
Students improvise simple harmonic accompaniments.

Objective

■ Students will improvise a harmonic accompaniment on open strings using tonic and dominant chord tones.

Materials

■ "Jig," in *New Tunes for Strings,* Book 1, by Stanley Fletcher, instructional design by Paul Rolland (New York: Boosey & Hawkes, 1971)

■ Piano

Prior Knowledge and Experiences

■ Students can recognize tonic and dominant chords by ear.

■ Students can play pizzicato and with the bow.

Procedures

1. Have students listen to the melody of "Jig" as you play it on the piano or a solo instrument.

2. Play the piece again, this time with harmonic accompaniment.

3. Have students walk in a circle to the pulse of the piece, walking one direction for tonic and then reversing direction for dominant.

4. Play the piece again and have students sing *do* on each beat when they hear the tonic and *sol* on each beat when they hear the change to the dominant while they are walking.

5. Ask students to take their instruments and return to a circle, this time making the circle larger. While you play the melody, have students play *do* or *sol* pizzicato on each beat on the open strings corresponding to the *do* and *sol* they sang while walking in the circle.

6. Back in their chairs, have individual students, now using their bows, try to create rhythm patterns to play for this tonic and dominant accompaniment. Then, while you play the melody, have students improvise rhythm patterns on the tonic and dominant as an accompaniment using their bows.

Indicators of Success

■ Students play the tonic and dominant accompaniment in various rhythm patterns while making the change from tonic to dominant appropriately.

Follow-up

■ Using Jacques Offenbach's "Barcarolle," have students create a similar harmonic accompaniment with the tonic and dominant pitches.

STANDARD 3B

STRATEGY 1 of 2

Improvising melodies, variations, and accompaniments: Students improvise melodic embellishments and simple rhythmic and melodic variations on given pentatonic melodies and melodies in major keys.

Objective

- Students will add rhythmic and melodic embellishments to a simple fiddle tune.

Materials

- Familiar fiddle tune "Boil Them Cabbage Down"
- Chalkboard

Prior Knowledge and Experiences

- Students can play a D major tetrachord and various rhythms.

Procedures

1. Teach students the tune "Boil Them Cabbage Down" by ear. Then write the basic melody on the chalkboard in half notes.

2. Have students play the tune with each of the following rhythmic variations:

3. Choose one of the patterns, and have the students play it with open A sounding throughout, creating double stops as the first embellishment:

4. Write a new rhythm pattern on the board, such as in the following example, and have students decide on pitches for the sixteenth-note sets.

5. Write the notes on the board, including the pitches that the students select for the sixteenth-note sets, and have the class play the tune. For example:

6. Have the entire class play the same notes on beats one and three, improvising on beats two and four, allowing all students to improvise together.

Indicators of Success

■ Students improvise rhythmic and melodic variations to "Boil Them Cabbage Down."

Follow-up

■ Have students improvise similar variations on other fiddle tunes.

■ Have individual students do solo improvisations in various sections of the piece.

■ Change the guideline for improvisation; for example, have students play the same notes on beat one, improvising on beats two, three, and four.

Improvising melodies, variations, and accompaniments: Students improvise melodic embellishments and simple rhythmic and melodic variations on given pentatonic melodies and melodies in major keys.

Objective

- Students will improvise rhythmic variations on a given melody in a major key.

Materials

- "Twinkle, Twinkle Little Star," in *Suzuki Violin School,* vol. 1, by Shinichi Suzuki (Secaucus, NJ: Summy-Birchard, 1978)
- Piano

Prior Knowledge and Experiences

- Students can play all the rhythmic variations of "Twinkle" as published in the Suzuki literature.
- Students have improvised rhythmic responses on open strings D and A in response to the teacher's call.

Procedures

1. Have the entire group play the first two phrases of "Twinkle," Variation A, in the Suzuki literature.

2. Have students identify the response, or answer section, as the second phrase they played.

3. Play the call (first phrase) on your instrument and have the class play the response (second phrase).

4. Have students vary the rhythm on at least one of the pitches of the response, using another "Twinkle" rhythm or one of their own. Allow all of them to respond together to your call.

5. As you play Variation A on the piano (to keep the rhythmic and harmonic context consistent), have the group play the call and have individual students improvise their responses.

Indicators of Success

- Students individually vary the rhythm of at least one pitch in the response after the group plays the call.

Follow-up

- Apply the same procedure to another piece (for example, "Long, Long Ago," in *Suzuki Violin School,* vol. 1 (Secaucus, NJ: Summy-Birchard, 1978).

- Have students individually vary the rhythm of two, three, and then four pitches in the response.

- Have individual students play the call and other students play the response.

STANDARD 4A

Composing and arranging music within specified guidelines: Students compose short pieces within specified guidelines, demonstrating how the elements of music are used to achieve unity and variety, tension and release, and balance.

Objective

- Students will compose, notate, and play a group piece that includes unity and variety and varying dynamics.

Materials

- Chalkboard

Prior Knowledge and Experiences

- Students have studied and played major and minor scales and triads.

Procedures

1. Tell students that they are going to compose a piece about a mosquito flying through a horizontal line that you have drawn on the chalkboard. Have students imagine the mosquito flying toward the line. As the mosquito approaches the line, it becomes wavy from the mosquito's point of view. Then, as the mosquito flies through the line to go out the other side of the chalkboard, the line becomes grainy and looks like dots from the mosquito's point of view. As the mosquito flies out the other side of the chalkboard and away from the line, the view is reversed.

2. Have students brainstorm about sounds they could use to represent the mosquito (tremolo, rubbing bow against strings, etc.) as it is flying and its view is changing. For example, when the line looks wavy to the mosquito, students could bend pitches; when the line is just dots, students could play pizzicato.

3. Discuss with students the repeating and contrasting elements in their "flight of the mosquito" composition. Have students decide the notation to use and then notate on paper.

4. Have students revise and augment their composition, decide on a title, and add dynamics.

5. Have students write program notes and play the composition.

Indicators of Success

- All students participate in composing, notating, and performing a piece that includes repeating and contrasting parts and varying dynamics.

Follow-up

- Have students compose another piece by choosing an idea (for example, a rocket takeoff and landing or a volcanic eruption), creating sounds, notating the sounds, organizing the piece, and performing it.

Composing and arranging music within specified guidelines: Students use a variety of traditional and nontraditional sound sources and electronic media when composing and arranging.

Objective

- Working in small groups, students will compose, and then notate and perform, a short piece using a variety of sounds produced on their instruments.

Materials

- Manuscript paper

Prior Knowledge and Experiences

- Students know how to play open strings and at least one finger on each string.

Procedures

1. Review rhythmic and melodic patterns students have learned. Play four-beat patterns and have students echo them on their instruments. (Or, have students play written patterns.)

2. Have students explore a variety of sounds that are possible on stringed instruments, including pizzicato, *col legno, ponticello,* glissando, and nonpitched sounds, such as knocking on the wood.

3. Divide students into small groups and ask each group to create a short piece. Give them guidelines appropriate to their skill level, such as:

   a. Limiting the pitch range

   b. Keeping the piece to a certain length (four to eight measures)

   c. Offering programmatic suggestions (for example, "jumping music," "calm music," "a piece about a cat")

   d. Including nonpitched sounds

   e. Suggesting that they compose music to accompany a particular story or a short poem

4. Have students write their compositions using either standard notation or a system they invent to remember their piece.

5. Have each group perform their composition for the class.

Indicators of Success

- Students discover a variety of sounds they can produce on their instruments and use them in their compositions.

- Students successfully notate their compositions and perform them, first within their groups and then for others.

Follow-up

- Have students perform the compositions for their general music class or homeroom or on a concert.

- Have students describe the ideas and processes they used to create their compositions. This will help them analyze their own creativity and indicate their respect for each other's ideas.

- Create a model composition as a class. Assign students to learn to play the composition as homework.

- Instead of having students notate the composition, allow them to perform from memory or by rote.

STANDARD 4C

Composing and arranging music within specified guidelines: Students use a variety of traditional and nontraditional sound sources and electronic media when composing and arranging.

Objective

■ Students will score a horror-film scene using special effects on their instruments, silence, and irregular rhythms to build suspense and resolve tension.

Materials

■ Narrative story or screenplay, with copies for each student, or silent video footage (about two minutes or less) with summary of events on handouts.

Prior Knowledge and Experiences

■ Students have played their instruments for at least eight weeks.

■ Students have explored advanced techniques, disguised as special-effects sounds.

Procedures

1. Review various special-effects sounds by having students play them: tremolo, snap pizzicato, glissandi using harmonics, bowing behind bridge, *col legno,* trill, fingered tremolo, various tapping sounds on body of instrument. Assist students in using good technique to produce the sounds.

2. Discuss the emotional or dramatic content or suggestion of each sound.

3. Read the selected story aloud or watch the selected video. If using a story or a screenplay, be sure each student has a copy, with lines spaced to allow room for editing musical ideas. If using a video, give students a handout with a summary of events.

4. Discuss the kinds of sounds or sound combinations that would enhance the drama of the scene. Point out the use of silence in horror films (for example, *Alien*), and tell students to use a silence of two seconds or more somewhere in their composition.

5. Have students create their composition using their own notational symbols.

6. Have students use the remaining class time and the next class session to work and rehearse. (The following class period is the "haunt-cert.")

Indicators of Success

■ Students create a score using a variety of sounds (both percussive and melodic) that build suspense and resolve tension and at least one silence of more than two seconds.

Follow-up

■ Show a portion of a horror film and ask students to identify techniques used by the composer to achieve suspense.

STANDARD 5A

Reading and notating music: Students read whole, half, quarter, eighth, sixteenth, and dotted notes and rests in 2/4, 3/4, 4/4, 6/8, 3/8, and alla breve meter signatures.

Objective

- Students will identify, recite, and perform a given rhythm pattern including whole, dotted-half, half, quarter, and eighth notes and rests in 2/4, 3/4, and 4/4 meter signatures.

Materials

- Two-measure rhythm patterns (on handouts or chalkboard)—including whole, dotted-half, half, quarter, and eighth notes and rests in 2/4, 3/4, and 4/4 meter signatures—teacher-generated or excerpted from a rhythm studies publication

Prior Knowledge and Experiences

- Students can identify and give rhythmic values of whole, dotted-half, half, quarter, and eighth notes and rests in 2/4, 3/4, and 4/4 meter signatures.

Procedures

1. Have students analyze a two-measure rhythm pattern (on handouts or chalkboard) to determine that the quarter note is the basic pulse and to determine how many pulses each measure contains.

2. Ask students to examine the entire pattern and verbally identify all rhythmic values—notes and rests—that are used.

3. Have students produce the rhythm pattern verbally by reciting note and rest values at a steady pulse, using any counting system. For example:

half note,   half note,   quarter,   quarter,   rest,   quarter,   etc.

4. Ask students to perform the pattern with their bows on their shoulders or in tubes (shadow bowing).

5. Have students perform the pattern on a designated open string.

6. Repeat steps 1–5 with other rhythm patterns.

Indicators of Success

- Students accurately identify, recite, and perform rhythm patterns of notes and rests at a steady pulse.

Follow-up

- Have students perform the example with uniform bow direction.
- Relate division of the bow to note values (i.e., whole bow for whole notes, half bow for half notes, etc.).

Reading and notating music: Students read at sight simple melodies in both the treble and bass clefs.

Objective

- Students will sightread melodies in simple keys with accurate rhythm, basic dynamics, and a minimal number of note errors.

Materials

- Any piece of music at least one level below the group's performance level

Prior Knowledge and Experiences

- Students can read music in the primary clef for their instruments.
- Students can identify simple meter and key signatures.

Procedures

1. Have students look over the new piece to be sightread. Have them identify the meter signature; identify the key signature, including checking the final note and accidentals to distinguish major from minor; check for repeats, fermatas, tempo changes, and dynamics; and locate possible difficult passages.

2. Discuss with the students the primary importance of rhythm, asking them, "Can music consist of rhythm only?" Ask students to give examples. Remind students that rhythm is the heart of music and that their top priority should be playing the rhythm with a steady beat without stopping.

3. Have students play only the rhythm of the piece; assign parts corresponding to the tonic chord. (This system is much more musical than playing the rhythm on open strings or on the same unison pitch.)

4. Have students shadow bow the piece (follow their part and play silently in the air). Since keeping the pulse is crucial, encourage students to tap their toes inside their shoes. Explain that in sightreading, bowing direction, fingerings, and occasional wrong notes are not of primary importance.

5. Have students play the piece without stopping. Reinforce rhythmic accuracy and praise students who did not stop even after they had made a mistake.

Indicators of Success

- Students sightread with greater accuracy, confidence, and rhythmic decisiveness.

Follow-up

- Have students continue to practice sightreading new music using these same procedures at least once a week; gradually increase the difficulty level.
- Add the expectation of reading the dynamics and bowings in sightreading.

Reading and notating music: Students read at sight simple melodies in both the treble and bass clefs.

Objective

■ Students will sing and play a short melody at sight with correct pitch and rhythm.

Materials

■ Any method book

Prior Knowledge and Experiences

■ Students have learned to read and play music with open strings and simple scale patterns with quarter, half, and whole notes.

■ Students have had experience sightsinging simple melodies in rhythm.

Procedures

1. Select a short melody from new material in the lesson book. Set the tempo and establish the first pitch.

2. Ask students to say the letter names in rhythm while pointing to the notes in the book.

3. Have students sing the pitches in rhythm using letter names while pointing to the notes. Help students with pitches when necessary.

4. Ask students to sing the pitches of the melody again in rhythm while they play the melody pizzicato with their instruments in playing position.

5. Have students hold their instruments, finger the notes on the fingerboard, and shadow bow the melody (follow their parts and play silently in the air) while singing the pitches in rhythm.

6. Ask students to place the bow on the string and play the piece with accurate pitch and rhythm using correct fingering. Have students continue singing the pitches, if you wish. If students have difficulty with this step, ask half the class to play the notes while the other half sings the letter names of the notes; then reverse their roles.

Indicators of Success

■ Students sightsing a melody with accurate pitch, note names, and rhythms.

■ Students play the same melody with accurate pitch and rhythm.

Follow-up

■ Have students use the same procedure to learn other new melodies. This is particularly helpful in learning new finger patterns and playing in new keys.

■ Ask students to study a four- or eight-measure example silently and to indicate when they are ready to play it. Then ask them to play the example.

STANDARD 5C

Reading and notating music: Students identify and define standard notation symbols for pitch, rhythm, dynamics, tempo, articulation, and expression.

Objective

- Students will identify and define accurately standard notation symbols and terms for pitch, rhythm, dynamics, tempo, articulation, and expression.

Materials

- Bingo boards created by students (8-1/2 x 11 inch paper, ruled off in five rows of five squares, each containing a term or symbol randomly selected from a list of at least thirty such terms and symbols appropriate for the students' skill level)
- Small (half-inch-square) paper or other markers to cover squares on bingo boards
- Music terms and symbols and their meanings written on cards for the caller

Prior Knowledge and Experiences

- Students understand the meaning of basic music terminology and symbols.

Procedures

1. Pass out markers to students for their bingo boards.

2. Explain that students should place a marker on each term or symbol on their boards as the term or symbol and its definition are called.

3. Select cards randomly from the set of callers' cards and call out both the term or symbol and its definition (or ask a student to serve as caller).

4. When a student has five markers covered in a row, ask the student to read the winning words with correct pronunciation. You might also require students to give the definition to qualify as winners.

Indicators of Success

- Students achieve accuracy of at least 90 percent on a quiz, matching terms or symbols from the game with the definitions.

- Students recognize, define, and show their understanding of the terms and symbols through their performance as they encounter them in their orchestra music or method books.

Follow-up

- Have students play the game using basic note values or note names on treble or bass clef.

- Add advanced terminology as students encounter new terms and symbols in their orchestra music.

- In later rounds, have the caller give only the definition; students must know the appropriate term or symbol to cover for that definition.

Reading and notating music: Students use standard notation to record their musical ideas and the musical ideas of others.

Objective

- Students will hear a melody, play it on their instruments, and write it down on manuscript paper.

Materials

- Chalkboard with staff
- Manuscript paper

Prior Knowledge and Experiences

- Students have developed basic notational skills and can read music.

Procedures

1. Play a two-measure melody. Ask the students to sing the melody on "la."

2. Sing the first note and ask the students to find that note on their instruments. Ask the first student who locates the pitch to tell the others what the note is.

3. Have students listen to the melody again and then try to find it on their instruments. Repeat this process as needed, offering individual assistance as you walk around the room.

4. Help students determine the key and meter signatures by reviewing the following concepts:

   a. Most tonal melodies end on the key note.

   b. The downbeats of measures are stressed in most phrases.

5. Using the students' responses, put the clef, key, and meter signature on the staffed chalkboard and have students put them on their manuscript paper. Ask students to write out the melody on their manuscript paper. Have one student write the melody on the chalkboard.

6. Have the class play what is written on the board, and then ask if it is correct. If it is not, ask a student to revise the melody written on the board.

7. Have students correct their melody and play from their own manuscript paper.

Indicators of Success

- Students listen to a melody, sing it back, write it correctly, and then play it.

Follow-up

- Continue this procedure at least once a week, increasing the length and difficulty of excerpts as appropriate.

- Have a student play a short melody that the class will sing, notate, and play.

Reading and notating music: Students use standard notation to record their musical ideas and the musical ideas of others.

Objective

- Students will notate accurately a tune from a television commercial.

Materials

- Audio recording of excerpt from television commercial
- Chalkboard
- Manuscript paper
- Various percussion instruments or electronic keyboard capable of producing variety of percussion sounds

Prior Knowledge and Experiences

- Students can play simple tunes by ear.
- Students can notate simple tunes using standard notation.

Procedures

1. Have students listen to the excerpt from a television commercial. Following an inevitable discussion about the product, play the excerpt again.
2. Ask students to sing back the tune. Then ask them to try playing it on their instruments.
3. After a few minutes of experimentation, call on a student who can play the melody. Ask the student to play the melody for the class and to write it on the chalkboard. Have the student verify pitch and rhythm of the notation by playing it back on his or her instrument.
4. On manuscript paper, have all students notate the tune in the clef for their instruments.
5. Have students play the excerpt in unison.

Indicators of Success

- Students notate the melody of the excerpt accurately for their instruments.

Follow-up

- Have students add sounds of percussion instruments to the unison playing of the excerpt, creating a new arrangement of the melody.
- Have students combine several tunes notated from commercials to make a composition.
- Encourage students to write down other tunes they hear, perhaps short motifs used in video games.
- Ask for volunteers to provide a simple harmonic accompaniment to the melody.

Reading and notating music: Students use standard notation to record their musical ideas and the musical ideas of others.

Objective

- Students will notate accurately short musical examples performed on a stringed instrument or on a piano.

Materials

- Manuscript paper
- Four-measure melody to be used for dictation (see figure 2)
- Piano (optional)

Prior Knowledge and Experiences

- Students can sing and read music using a system of tonal syllables or letter names.
- Each student can notate the clef for his or her instrument, bar lines, meter signatures, and key signatures.

Procedures

1. Identify the meter signature and key signature of the melody to be dictated and ask students to draw them on their manuscript paper. Also, have each student draw the appropriate clef for his or her instrument.

2. Direct students to mark off four measures of equal length on the blank staff with the appropriate numbers marked above each measure to represent beats, as in figure 1.

3. Have students set a steady beat by patsching on one leg, tapping their foot, or using another method. Perform the four-measure melody on a stringed instrument or on the piano. On the first hearing, have the students attempt to mark the rhythm above the four measures on their staff, using horizontal lines above the numbers they have written to indicate the duration and number of notes they heard (see figure 2).

4. On the second hearing, have students check the accuracy of the rhythm they have written by quietly tapping it with their index finger. For students who are still unsure of the rhythm, repeat the melody.

5. On the third or subsequent hearing, tell the students the tonal syllable of the first note. Ask students to mark the first letters of the appropriate tonal syllables above the horizontal lines they drew for rhythm. (See figure 2; although the example indicates the use of tonic *sol-fa*, another system of tonal syllables or letter names may be used.) Have students play back their own notation, using their own instruments.

6. Ask students to transfer their own notation into standard notation.

7. Have students play the melody they have written in standard notation.

Indicators of Success

- Students notate simple melodies using horizontal lines for rhythmic duration and tonal syllables or letter names for pitches.
- Students notate simple melodies using standard notation.

Follow-up

- As students become more skilled at music notation, have them use standard notation as the melody is dictated.
- Ask individual students to compose a melody, notate it, and play it for the class. Ask the class to notate the student's melody.

Figure 1

Figure 2

STANDARD 5E

Reading and notating music: Students sightread, accurately and expressively, music with a level of difficulty of 2, on a scale of 1 to 6.

Objective

- In an instrumental work with a level of difficulty of 2, students will sightread specific rhythm patterns and perform them accurately.

Materials

- "Fanfare for Strings" by Doris Gazda (San Diego: Neil A. Kjos Music Company, 1994), Level 2
- Chalkboard
- Manuscript paper
- Handouts of rhythm sheet with nine rhythm patterns from "Fanfare for Strings" (see accompanying figure)

Prior Knowledge and Experiences

- Students have worked on rhythmic reading and awareness of other orchestral parts being performed in their ensemble.

Procedures

1. On the chalkboard, notate the nine rhythm patterns that occur in "Fanfare for Strings" (see accompanying figure). Write in counting symbols. Give students handouts of the rhythm sheet and have them write in counting symbols.

2. Have students sightread each rhythm pattern by speaking the counting symbols and clapping the beat.

3. Ask students to look at their orchestra parts for "Fanfare for Strings" and identify exactly where each rhythm pattern occurs (if it does) in their part, writing the appropriate measure numbers on their rhythm sheet.

4. Using the handouts again, lead the class through the rhythm patterns, clapping and speaking. Ask students to identify where the patterns occur in the music and in which instruments' parts.

Indicators of Success

- Students visually recognize and identify rhythms when they hear them played.

- Students read similar rhythms at sight with accuracy of at least 80 percent.

Follow-up

- Have students perform "Fanfare for Strings" with special attention to rhythmic accuracy while listening to the rhythm patterns in other parts being played in the ensemble.

- Have students write counting symbols under rhythm patterns in new music.

1. $\frac{4}{4}$ ♩ ♫ ♩ ♩ | ♩. 𝄽 |

2. $\frac{4}{4}$ 𝅗𝅥 𝅗𝅥 | 𝅝 |

3. $\frac{4}{4}$ 𝅗𝅥 ♩ ♩ | 𝅝 |

4. $\frac{4}{4}$ ♩ ♩ ♩ ♩ | 𝅝 |

5. $\frac{4}{4}$ ♩. ♩ | 𝅗𝅥 𝅗𝅥 |

6. $\frac{4}{4}$ 𝅝  | 𝅗𝅥 ▬ |

7. $\frac{4}{4}$ 𝄽 ♫ ♩ ♩ | ♩ ♩ ♩ ♩ |

8. $\frac{4}{4}$ 𝄽 ♫ ♩ ♩ | ▬ |

9. $\frac{4}{4}$ ▬ 𝅗𝅥 | ♩ ♩ ♩ ♩ |

STANDARD 6A

Listening to, analyzing, and describing music: Students describe specific music events in a given aural example, using appropriate terminology.

Objective

■ Through listening, students will identify phrases and sections in pieces in AB and ABA form.

Materials

■ Recording of a traditional song that alternates between verse and chorus

■ Orchestral arrangement of a minuet and trio from students' folders

■ Recording of another minuet and trio

■ Chalkboard

■ Audio-playback equipment

Prior Knowledge and Experiences

■ Students have been learning to play a minuet and trio.

■ Students understand ABA song form through previous analysis.

Procedures

1. Play the recording of a traditional song in two-part form (AB)—for example, "Battle Hymn of the Republic" or "Home on the Range"—and have students identify where the various repetitions occur within the piece. Point out that the names for the sections are "verse" and "chorus." On the chalkboard, have students help you diagram the piece by calling the verses "A" and the choruses "B." Explain the usefulness of being able to recognize the sections of a piece.

2. Using a minuet and trio that the students have been learning, have the students play to the end of each section and stop.

3. Discuss these divisions and then have students help you diagram the form (ABA) on the board.

4. Play a recording of a minuet and trio that the students have not heard before. Have them raise their left hand when the B section begins and their right hand when the A section returns.

5. Have students again play the minuet and trio all the way through.

Indicators of Success

■ Students identify the sections of a piece in two-part form and the sections of minuet and trio form.

Follow-up

■ In rehearsing other music, refer to the sections (A, B, minuet, or trio) rather than rehearsal numbers or letters (for example, "Begin at the trio").

■ Use similar procedures for analyzing new music that is in theme-and-variations or rondo form.

STANDARD 6B

Listening to, analyzing, and describing music: Students analyze the uses of elements of music in aural examples representing diverse genres and cultures.

Objective

- Students will analyze the AABA form of a popular song and compare it to a Classical piece in the same form.

Materials

- Classical piece in AABA form from students' folders
- Recording of a popular song in AABA form
- Audio-playback equipment
- Chalkboard

Prior Knowledge and Experiences

- Students can play the Classical piece well.

Procedures

1. Play the recording of a popular song. Tell students the song consists of two sections, A and B, and the first section will be called "A." Before playing the recording again, ask students to stand up when the A section begins, sit down when it ends, and then stand again if and when they hear the A section again. (Students should sit at the end of the first A section, stand immediately for the second A section, sit during the B section, and stand again for the final A section.)

2. Ask a student to come to the chalkboard. Play the recording again, having the students stand up and sit down as instructed in step 1. Have the student at the chalkboard write A or B on the board as signaled by the students, resulting in AABA.

3. Ask students to play their Classical piece, standing and sitting as in steps 1 and 2. Have a student at the chalkboard write A or B on the board as signaled by the students.

4. Ask students why they think AABA form is so common in music.

5. Have students play the piece again, standing again whenever the A section returns.

Indicators of Success

- Students identify AABA form in popular music that they hear and Classical music that they play.

Follow-up

- Apply this procedure to other music the students play, with forms such as minuet and trio or simple rondo form (ABACA).
- Have students listen to recordings of music in other forms, such as minuet and trio or simple rondo, and apply the same procedure.

STANDARD 6C

STRATEGY 1 of 2

Listening to, analyzing, and describing music: Students demonstrate knowledge of
the basic principles of meter, rhythm, tonality, intervals, chords, and
harmonic progressions in their analyses of music.

Objective

- Students will identify and sing the intervals in a unison passage of a piece they know well by ear.

Materials

- Recording of Serenade, K. 525, *Eine kleine Nachtmusik* by Wolfgang Amadeus Mozart
- Melody of the first four measures of the piece written in each clef on the chalkboard
- Music for *Eine kleine Nachtmusik* (if available)

Prior Knowledge and Experiences

- Students have previously listened to *Eine kleine Nachtmusik*.
- Students have identified all the intervals within a major scale, visually and aurally, and can play and sing them, given a starting pitch.

Procedures

1. Play the recording of *Eine kleine Nachtmusik,* stopping at the first cadence.
2. Direct students' attention to the melody on the chalkboard. Have students sing the melody and then identify the intervals.
3. Have students play these four measures, listening particularly for the sounds of the intervals as they perform.
4. Play the recording of the entire first movement, having the students follow their parts in their printed music (if available).

Indicators of Success

- Students correctly sing and identify the intervals in the first four measures of Mozart's *Eine kleine Nachtmusik*.

Follow-up

- Using the first few measures of other well-known Classical pieces—such as Andante from Symphony no. 94 ("Surprise") by Joseph Haydn or the first movement of Symphony no. 5 by Ludwig van Beethoven—follow a similar procedure to develop interval identification skills.

Listening to, analyzing, and describing music: Students demonstrate knowledge of the basic principles of meter, rhythm, tonality, intervals, chords, and harmonic progressions in their analyses of music.

Objective

- Students will identify aurally changes in tonality from major to minor.

Materials

- Andante from Symphony no. 94 in G ("Surprise") by Joseph Haydn, arr. Sandra Dackow (Cleveland: Ludwig Music Publishing Company, 1989), Level 3

- "Themes from the Moldau" by Bedrich Smetana, arr. Robert S. Frost (Delevan, NY: Kendor Music, 1982), Level 3

- Chalkboard (with measures 3–7 and first four measures of the coda of "Themes from the Moldau" written on staff)

Prior Knowledge and Experiences

- Students can play simple melodies, including songs such as "Hot Cross Buns" and "At Pierrot's Door," by ear.

- Students have learned to play "Surprise" Symphony and "Themes from the Moldau."

- Students can play a major and a minor scale.

Procedures

1. Have students play the first four measures of "Surprise" Symphony. Then have them play measures 41–44. Ask them to describe the differences between these two excerpts.

2. Have students play "Hot Cross Buns," followed by "Burned Hot Cross Buns" (same song in minor key). Ask students which note in the scale determines whether it is major or minor tonality. (It is the third note.)

3. Play "At Pierrot's Door" and ask students to echo the melody. Ask if anyone can demonstrate how to make it minor. Play this song as a group in major and then in minor tonality. Then, play one version or the other and ask students whether it is major or minor.

4. Have the first-violin section play "Themes from the Moldau," measures 3–7 and the first four measures of the coda. Ask the class to sing the theme (on a neutral syllable or with letter names), first in major, then in minor, reading the pitches from the chalkboard.

5. Ask everyone to close their eyes except the first-violin section. Silently, show the first-violin section which measures to play, either measures 3–7 or the coda, and have them play it. Then have the other students identify which one they played and whether it was major or minor.

6. Have all students play through "Themes from the Moldau," standing when the major section begins.

7. Use the same procedure for "Surprise" Symphony. (*Note:* This piece begins in major and changes to minor. You may wish to have students begin seated and then stand when the minor section begins.)

(continued)

Indicators of Success

- Students accurately identify major and minor tonalities and change, as appropriate, from one to the other in their playing.

Follow-up

- Have students listen to the second movement of Symphony no. 1 by Gustav Mahler. Ask them to identify the folk song ("Frère Jacques") and the tonality (minor). Have students play "Frère Jacques" by rote, in D major and then in D minor.

STANDARD 7A

STRATEGY 1 of 2

Evaluating music and music performances: Students develop criteria for evaluating the quality and effectiveness of music performances and compositions and apply the criteria in their personal listening and performing.

Objective

■ Students will identify and perform a phrase without expression and one with expression and develop criteria to evaluate the two versions.

Materials

■ Any concert piece or étude that contains complete melodic phrases for each part

■ Chalkboard

Prior Knowledge and Experiences

■ Students have learned how to play the notes in the musical selection.

Procedures

1. Perform a phrase from the selected piece for the class, first without expression and then with expression.

2. Ask students which version they preferred.

3. Have individual students imitate the example without expression and then with expression.

4. Have the entire class perform both versions of the phrase. Ask students why they preferred the version with expression. Then discuss with them criteria for evaluating the quality or effectiveness of music they hear and play. Write these criteria on the chalkboard.

5. Lead the orchestra in playing the rest of the piece, section by section. At the end of each section, ask students to evaluate that section based on the criteria written on the chalkboard.

Indicators of Success

■ Students perform phrases with expression.

Follow-up

■ Introduce a new piece that is not technically challenging. Ask students to study their parts silently, noting the dynamics. Ask students to sightread the piece with dynamics and expression.

■ Add to and refine the criteria students have developed. Have students use these criteria to evaluate the quality and effectiveness of music played in subsequent classes.

Evaluating music and music performances: Students develop criteria for evaluating the quality and effectiveness of music performances and compositions and apply the criteria in their personal listening and performing.

Objective

- Students will devise a form for use in evaluating their own and their classmates' performances.

Materials

- Chalkboard

Prior Knowledge and Experiences

- Students have prepared assigned musical excerpts for solo performance and evaluation.

Procedures

1. Discuss skills students have learned on their instruments. Write the students' responses on the board.

2. Ask students, "How do these skills help you make music?" Guide the students to musical answers, such as rhythmic flow, intonation, melodic expression, and phrasing. Write the students' responses on the board.

3. Ask students, "What should the listener be able to hear in your playing, based on what you have learned?" Help students identify the most important skills that have been emphasized in class, such as steady tempo, accurate intonation, and beautiful tone. Write the students' responses on the board.

4. Using the lists on the board, have students work with you to create an evaluation form to use for performance tests this year. Help them keep in mind the limited amount of time for each person's performance (for example, two minutes) and for evaluation.

5. Develop criteria for constructive criticism—instead of saying something is wrong, suggest how it can be corrected or improved.

Indicators of Success

- Students develop appropriate evaluative criteria.
- Students develop an attitude of cooperation with each other.

Follow-up

- After two rounds of testing, reexamine the form and make any necessary adjustments, informing students of the reasons for making the changes.

STANDARD 7B

Evaluating music and music performances: Students evaluate the quality and effectiveness of their own and others' performances, compositions, arrangements, and improvisations by applying specific criteria appropriate for the style of the music and offer constructive suggestions for improvement.

Objective

■ Students will evaluate class-mates' performances and write constructive criticism.

Materials

■ Copies of critique forms developed by students in a previous class.

Prior Knowledge and Experiences

■ Students have prepared assigned musical excerpts for solo performance/evaluation.

Procedures

1. Pass out copies of critique forms developed by students and review the criteria with the class. Remind students of the meaning of constructive criticism—instead of saying something is wrong, suggest how it can be corrected or improved.

2. As each student plays the excerpt to be evaluated, have the others watch, listen, and write comments. When each performer finishes, ask students to complete their written evaluation of the performance.

3. On your own form, evaluate, for a grade, each performance along with the students.

4. After everyone has played, have students turn in their critiques. Screen them before distributing them to the other students.

5. Lead a short discussion, verbally critiquing outstanding perfor-mances and discussing common errors.

Indicators of Success

■ In their evaluations of classmates' performances, students focus on details of technique, offer insightful comments to classmates, and use language that indicates respect and a cooperative attitude.

Follow-up

■ Using a standard adjudication form (from a state festival, for example), have students perform for and then critique each other.

STANDARD 8B

Understanding relationships between music, the other arts, and disciplines outside the arts:
*Students describe ways in which the principles and subject matter of other disciplines
taught in the school are interrelated with those of music.*

Objective

- Students will identify elementary terms and principles of acoustics as they relate to beginning harmonics on a stringed instrument and find, perform, and identify simple natural harmonics.

Materials

- Any string method book that introduces harmonics
- Numerous written examples of individual natural harmonics
- Chalkboard

Prior Knowledge and Experiences

- Students can perform basic major scales accurately with good intonation and hand position.
- Students are advanced enough to perform Level 2 music.
- Students' bow control is fairly consistent.

Procedures

1. Demonstrate several natural harmonics on a stringed instrument. Explain that in today's lesson students will learn to find and produce these sounds.

2. Place the following terms on the board and discuss their definitions, drawing appropriate diagrams.

   a. Physics: The science that deals with matter and motion.

   b. Acoustics: The science of sound, which is a branch of physics, including the production, transmission, and effects of sound.

   c. Sound: The sensation of hearing vibrating energy. In music, a tone.

   d. Vibrations: A periodic motion of the particles of an elastic body, such as a string, in alternately opposite directions from a state of balance (equilibrium) when that equilibrium has been disturbed, as when a stretched string produces a musical sound. (Draw vibrating string lengths on the board.)

   e. Node: A point of a vibrating string length marked by absolute or relative freedom from vibratory motion. (Show nodes on the string lengths drawn on the board.)

   f. Harmonics: A flute-like tone produced on a stringed instrument by touching a vibrating string at a node point.

3. Explain that natural harmonics work on the principle of vibrating string lengths as described above. Harmonics are a natural phenomenon in physics and acoustics. Dividing a string in halves, thirds, fourths, and so on at nodal points produces natural harmonics. Have students examine their stringed instruments and determine where the halfway point is on a string (midway between the bridge and the nut); have the students try to produce this basic harmonic while maintaining good posture and hand position.

4. Show how placing a finger lightly on the string at the string's natural division, or nodal point, produces the harmonic. This causes the string to vibrate in segments instead of as a whole. The result is called a harmonic, a partial, or an overtone. Help students find the right place and acquire the right finger touch to produce the proper harmonic.

5. Explain that touching the string at its midpoint makes the harmonic one octave above the fundamental open string. Perform these pitches with a stringed instrument. Have the students sing the octave produced. Explain that placing the finger lightly at the quarter division point (show on string and on board diagram) produces a harmonic that sounds two octaves above the fundamental open string. Perform these sounds on the instrument. (Natural harmonics occur when a half is divided in half. Students can produce another harmonic three octaves above the fundamental by touching the string at the eighth division point.)

6. Explain and show the method of notation for natural harmonics (those derived from the open strings): write the notes actually sounded with a small circle over each or write diamond-head notes, indicating the nodal point to be touched. Show and demonstrate examples of each.

Indicators of Success

■ Students find and play simple natural harmonics of the first half and quarter of the string length on all open strings.

■ Students identify printed natural harmonics.

■ Students define the elementary terms of physics and acoustics.

Follow-up

■ Demonstrate a natural harmonic in which the string is divided into three segments resulting in a pitch that sounds a twelfth (octave and a fifth) above the open string. Have students note that this pitch can be produced by touching either point, a third of the distance from the bridge or a third of the distance from the nut.

■ Have students study and perform a simple composition using easy natural harmonics.

STANDARD 9A

Understanding music in relation to history and culture: Students describe distinguishing characteristics of representative music genres and styles from a variety of cultures.

Objective

- Students will identify instrumentation in and describe rhythmic characteristics of music from South Africa.

Materials

- Recording of *Synchro System,* performed by King Sunny Ade and His African Beats, Island Records 162-539737
- Teacher-made handouts of rhythm patterns from King Sunny Ade recording
- Pictures of South African instruments (if available)
- Audio-playback equipment

Prior Knowledge and Experiences

- Students have a basic knowledge of rhythms.
- Students have developed elementary critical listening skills.

Procedures

1. Play "Tolongo," from King Sunny Ade recording, asking students to listen for the instruments that are playing.

2. After they have heard the entire piece and identified the instruments, ask students questions about other things they have heard (for example, "Was there a melody?" "Describe the tempo"). Direct them to answer in musical terms, rather than with words such as "interesting" "exciting," or unusual."

3. Play the piece again, asking students to tap the beat on their desks, using only two fingers.

4. Ask students, "Was it easy to keep the beat?" Ask "Why?" or "Why not?"

5. Tap a predominant rhythm used in the music and have students tap it and then write it. Distribute the handouts with rhythm patterns; clap the rhythms and have students clap them.

6. Explain that the drums used on the recording are called "talking drums." Have students discuss why.

7. Directing students' attention to instruments, rhythm patterns, and other special characteristics in the music, have students listen to the piece a third time.

Indicators of Success

- Students identify specific characteristics of music of South Africa.

Follow-up

- Work with the social studies teacher to bring music into classes when the culture of South Africa is studied.
- Listen to the same recording and focus on the kinds of scales used. Ask the class to relate those scales to scales they play in orchestra.

STANDARD 9C

Understanding music in relation to history and culture: Students compare, in several cultures of the world, functions music serves, roles of musicians, and conditions under which music is typically performed.

Objective

■ Students will compare the function of music in Bulgaria with the function of music in the United States.

Materials

■ *Village Music of Bulgaria,* produced by Ethel Rain and Martin Koenig, Elektra/Nonesuch compact disc 79195-2

Prior Knowledge and Experiences

■ Students have listened to music of other countries to analyze instrumentation, rhythm patterns, and scales used.

Procedures

1. Play "Potajno Rada Godiya," from the recording *Village Music of Bulgaria.* Ask students to listen for the underlying feeling of the music.

2. After listening, ask students how the music makes them feel. Prompt them with questions such as, "Did it sound energetic? Anxious? Sad? Happy?"

3. Tell them the setting of the music—a wedding—and what function the music actually serves in the Bulgarian culture. (Historically, this music was performed for guests a week after the wedding ceremony when the newlyweds first visited the bride's parents. Though this ritual is no longer practiced, the music continues to be a part of Bulgarian culture and is performed today as a folk song.)

4. Lead a discussion of how music might be used in the United States in a similar situation. Ask the students, "Is there music in the United States written especially for weddings? Can you name any pieces?"

5. Ask questions that emphasize how people are connected through music, such as, "If you were at a wedding in Bulgaria, would you feel joy for the couple when you heard this music?" and "How do you think a Bulgarian boy or girl would feel visiting a wedding in the United States when 'Here Comes the Bride' started to play?"

6. Have students make a list of similarities and differences in the function of music of the United States and that of Bulgaria. (For example, in both countries, music plays a role in ceremonies such as weddings and funerals. In modern times, some Bulgarians sing songs to ask for the blessing of a rich harvest; Americans would not typically sing for this purpose. With the modernization of Bulgaria, the differences are not as dramatic as they were previously.)

Indicators of Success

■ Students describe similarities and differences between the music of Bulgaria and the music of the United States. Students learn that they are connected to other cultures through the underlying need for music.

■ Students learn that music is used for ceremonies in cultures throughout the world.

(continued)

Follow-up

- Find appropriate music of Bulgaria for the orchestra to play and discuss its function compared to music used in the United States (or another culture) for a similar function.

- Follow a similar procedure with music of other cultures.

- Have students research wedding music from other cultures.

STRATEGIES
Grades 9–12

Performing on instruments, alone and with others, a varied repertoire of music: Students perform on at least one instrument accurately and independently, alone and in small and large ensembles, with good posture, good playing position, and good breath, bow, or stick control. *

Objective

■ Students will identify aurally in-tune and out-of-tune pitches as they occur in the third and seventh degrees of the scale and learn to adjust them in relationship to the key or tonality in which they are playing.

Materials

■ *Suite for Strings* by Samuel Scheidt, arr. Robert Klotman (Van Nuys, CA: Alfred Publishing Company, 1982), Level 4

Prior Knowledge and Experiences

■ Students have learned all of the basic finger patterns in first position.

■ Students have played "Courante" from *Suite for Strings*.

Procedures

1. Have one student on violin, viola, or cello accurately tune his or her A, D, and G strings so that they are perfect fifths. Then have that student begin to play a D major scale starting on the open D string, stopping on the second note, E, and keeping the first finger in place.

2. Have the student play a double-stop with the open G string, without moving the first finger, creating a major sixth (G to E). The major sixth will need to be adjusted to bring it into tune. Ask the class what needs to be done to correct the pitch. (As the sixth note in the scale of G major, the E will need to be lowered slightly to bring the sixth into tune.) Have the student adjust the pitch of the E as needed and keep the finger in place.

3. Have the student play a double-stop with the open A string, without moving the first finger from its position, creating a perfect fourth (E to A). The perfect fourth will be out of tune—the E being flat—and the pitch of the E will need to be raised slightly. Be sure that students note that, depending on its position in the key or tonality, the note E has been located in three different places.

4. Discuss which half step is smaller in the major scale (from the third to the fourth degree of the scale or from the seventh to the eighth degree of the scale). In the process, explain the nature of the leading tone (the seventh degree), which has a strong tendency to lead up to the tonic.

5. Have all students tune all strings accurately, beginning on the lowest C on the instrument and concentrating on the difference between the half-step intervals from E to F and from B to C.

6. Have students identify B natural as the leading tone in C major, the key of the "Courante."

7. Have students play "Courante" from *Suite for Strings,* concentrating on raising each B natural, the seventh tone in the scale of C major, so that it leads the ear to the tonic, C.

(continued)

---

* This is Standard 2A for Grades 5–8. Students at the 9–12 level are expected to demonstrate higher levels of the skills that are listed, deal with more complex music, and respond to music in increasingly more sophisticated ways. The strategy presented here illustrates how the standard that is listed could be put into action in grades 9–12.

Indicators of Success

■ Students play "Courante" (which includes changes in tonality) with noticeable improvement in their intonation.

■ Students are able to explain which scale degrees they should raise or lower slightly.

Follow-up

■ In "Galliard Battaglia," from the same suite, have students adjust the tuning of the third and seventh scale degrees when they occur in the music.

■ In another piece, ask students to identify the key and play that scale in tune, with particular attention to the leading tone. Have students locate leading tones in their music and play the piece with accurate intonation.

STANDARD 2A

STRATEGY 2 of 2

Performing on instruments, alone and with others, a varied repertoire of music: Students perform on at least one instrument accurately and independently, alone and in small and large ensembles, with good posture, good playing position, and good breath, bow, or stick control. *

Objective

- Students will improve their rhythm and pitch accuracy in an orchestra piece, at the same time becoming more aware of their individual parts in relation to the full orchestration.

Materials

- A string orchestra piece that is new to the students

Prior Knowledge and Experiences

- Students have sightread the new piece at a previous rehearsal.

Procedure

1. Prepare students to rehearse the piece they have sightread previously by reviewing the meter signature, key signature, tempo, dynamics, and any other crucial information, such as repeat signs.

2. Explain that in the repetitions of the piece during this rehearsal, they should identify how the other parts relate to their own, considering questions such as "Which section has the same rhythm as ours?" or "Which section is playing during our rests?"

3. Have the orchestra play the entire piece (or a section of it, depending on the length of the piece).

4. Lead the orchestra in playing the piece or section again, this time asking the first violins to play arco and the rest of the orchestra to play pizzicato. Make any comments that are needed to help students correct rhythm, intonation, and bowing in the arco part.

5. Continue this process, asking the second violins (followed by the violas, then the cellos, then the basses) to play arco while the rest of the orchestra plays pizzicato.

6. Finally, ask the full orchestra to play arco, performing the entire piece or section as written, with attention to all musical aspects of the piece.

Indicators of Success

- Students perform the piece with accurate rhythm and pitch.
- Students are aware of how the other parts fit with their own part in the composition.

Follow-up

- Apply this technique to a section of any piece when individual parts need work. (This will allow you to focus on one section of the orchestra and keep all students included in the music.)

---

* This is Standard 2A for Grades 5–8. Students at the 9–12 level are expected to demonstrate higher levels of the skills that are listed, deal with more complex music, and respond to music in increasingly more sophisticated ways. The strategy presented here illustrates how the standard that is listed could be put into action in grades 9–12.

4577

7 STRINGS AND ORCHESTRA   67

STANDARD 2A

Performing on instruments, alone and with others, a varied repertoire of music: Students perform with expression and technical accuracy a large and varied repertoire of instrumental literature with a level of difficulty of 4, on a scale of 1 to 6.

Objective

■ Students will identify and execute bowing styles and other musical content, specifically tempo marking and rhythmic materials, and determine how they contribute to the differences in the expressive qualities between two contrasting movements of a standard work for string orchestra.

Materials

■ First movement ("Boisterous Bourrée") and third movement ("Sentimental Saraband"), from *Simple Symphony* by Benjamin Britten (London: Oxford University Press, 1963), Level 5

■ Chalkboard

Prior Knowledge and Experiences

■ Students are able to play the first and third movements of *Simple Symphony* from beginning to end, demonstrating technical skills needed for this piece, such as shifting, vibrato, and bowing skills.

■ Students can determine and perform appropriate bow strokes and articulation from notation.

Procedures

1. Review D minor and B-flat major scales. Demonstrate and have students imitate short melodic patterns in these keys. Use the bowings and articulations needed for first and third movements of the *Simple Symphony* (spiccato, *detach*é, hooked, *martelé;* legato and staccato). Review how each bowing is notated, drawing particular attention to Britten's practice of indicating hooked bowing using a horizontal bracket above the hooked notes.

2. Have students visually inspect their parts to locate different types of bowings that are used in each movement; have them play an excerpt that demonstrates each bowing. During this activity, list on the chalkboard the bowings used in each movement.

3. Discuss how the types of articulations indicated by Britten contribute to the expressive intent of each movement. For example, the Saraband contains very few repeated off-the-string notes and much use of legato *detaché* strokes; this contributes to its lyrical quality. The Bourrée has much spiccato and staccato playing, reflecting the "boisterous" character of the movement.

4. Have students again review their parts, locating the tempo indications used throughout each movement. List these terms on the board by movement (e.g., *allegro ritmico* in the first movement versus poco lento and *pesante* in the third movement).

5. Point out to students that the Bourrée has many rhythm patterns involving durations of less than a beat, whereas the Saraband has predominantly rhythmic values of a beat or longer. Discuss how these differences in tempo indications and in the structure of the rhythm patterns used by Britten contribute to differences in expressive qualities between the first and third movements.

Indicators of Success

■ Students accurately perform the two movements, demonstrating the instrumental techniques and expressive considerations of the two movements.

■ Students discuss how elements of bowing, tempo, and rhythmic content contribute to the different styles and expressive meanings of these two contrasting movements.

Follow-up

- Have students rewrite (or provide a handout for them) and perform the first theme of the Saraband movement (measures 1–5, first violin) in 3/8 as opposed to the original notation in 3/2. Discuss how this difference in notation, although not necessarily impacting on how the theme sounds, conveys a different expressive quality to experienced performers (specifically, a sustained connected style that contributes to the sentimental quality of the movement). Repeat this procedure, rewriting and performing the Bourrée movement in 4/2 instead of 2/2.

- Ask students to look up bourrée and saraband in reference materials such as *Baker's Biographical Dictionary of Musicians,* 8th ed., by Theodore Baker, rev. Nicholas Slonimsky (New York: G. Schirmer, 1992) or *The New Grove Dictionary of Music and Musicians,* Stanley Sadie, ed. (London: Macmillan Publishers, 1980) to find the characteristics of each dance. Ask them to consider how the title of each movement relates to *Simple Symphony*.

- Invite students to research Britten's life and discuss the fact that the *Simple Symphony* was constructed of melodies he wrote as a child.

Proficient

STANDARD 2C

**Performing on instruments, alone and with others, a varied repertoire of music:** Students perform in small ensembles with one student on a part.

Objective

- Students will play their parts in an orchestral piece independently and with rhythmic accuracy, good intonation, and ensemble precision (attacks, releases, and balance).

Materials

- Any piece for string orchestra
- Chalkboard

Prior Knowledge and Experiences

- Students are able to play their parts in the selected piece from beginning to end.

Procedures

1. Divide the orchestra into string quartets or quintets, explaining that each small ensemble will play for the remaining members of the orchestra after several sessions. For each group, identify or ask students to identify a leader to keep the group on task and report back to you. Rotate group leadership in subsequent sessions.

2. To prepare students for rehearsing in small groups, discuss appropriate behaviors for working together (e.g., showing respect for each other's opinions and cooperating with each other while rehearsing).

3. On the chalkboard, write criteria (such as rhythmic accuracy, intonation, dynamics, phrasing, style, precise attacks and releases, and good balance) and discuss each aspect with the class.

4. Using the selected piece, have students work in their ensembles, giving attention to each aspect listed on the board.

Indicators of Success

- Students play their own parts with greater awareness of the other parts and with more confidence and independence.

Follow-up

- Have each ensemble play for the class. Students may give constructive criticism on the performances, based on the stated criteria.

- Have group leaders keep a written record of what was accomplished in the session and submit their records to you to provide evidence of their progress and to provide focus for the next session.

- Have students evaluate expressive and technical qualities of each other's playing.

STANDARD 3A

Improvising melodies, variations, and accompaniments: Students improvise stylistically appropriate harmonizing parts.

Objective

■ Using a melody they notate through melodic dictation, students will improvise harmony parts in an appropriate style and compare their harmonizations with that of the composer's.

Materials

■ "Rhosymedre" by Ralph Vaughan Williams, arr. Arnold Foster (New York: Galaxy Music Company, 1938; distributed by ECS Publishing), Level 4

■ Manuscript paper

Prior Knowledge and Experiences

■ Students have experience with rhythmic and melodic dictation.

■ Students have experience improvising harmony parts to simple melodies.

Procedures

1. Teach students the hymn tune from "Rhosymedre" by rote—first have them sing it, and then have them play it. (*Note:* The hymn tune begins on the upbeat to measure 9 in the viola part.)

2. Have students take melodic dictation, notating the hymn tune in 4/4 meter in G major.

3. Ask students to rewrite the melody with a meter signature of 4/2, as Vaughan Williams wrote it.

4. Discuss the legato, sustained style of the hymn tune, noting that a harmonized part should also be legato in order to be consistent with the style.

5. Ask the violins and violas to play the melody and the cellos and basses to improvise harmony to the melody in the style of the hymn tune. Have students switch roles.

6. Distribute the parts for "Rhosymedre." Have students locate the hymn tune in their parts (first violin at measure 25). Have the orchestra play that section (upbeat to measure 25 to the downbeat of measure 40). Discuss Vaughan Williams's harmonization of the tune, having students compare the harmonization to their own.

Indicators of Success

■ Students listen to and notate a melody using melodic dictation.

■ Students improvise a harmony part to a given melody.

■ Students compare a composer's harmonization to their own.

(continued)

Follow-up

■ Use students' harmonization to the hymn tune but with a contrasting rhythmic style (for example, bossa nova, country western, or swing), perhaps including percussion accompaniment, live or with a drum machine or portable electronic keyboard.

■ Have students listen to Vaughan Williams's *English Folk Song Suite* (e.g., Cleveland Symphonic Winds, Frederick Fennell, Telarc compact disc 80099), written for military band. Have them notate the melody of the second movement. Discuss the composer's harmonization of the melody and compare it to his harmonization of "Rhosymedre."

■ Follow the same procedures using "Jesu, Joy of Man's Desiring" by J. S. Bach, arr. Reginald Jacques (Carey, NC: Oxford University Press, 1949), Level 4.

■ Teach "Simple Gifts" by rote and have the orchestra improvise an accompaniment.

STANDARD 3B

Improvising melodies, variations, and accompaniments: Students improvise rhythmic and melodic variations on given pentatonic melodies and melodies in major and minor keys.

Objective

- Students will improvise rhythmic and melodic variations on a traditional fiddle tune in an appropriate style and improvise an appropriate accompaniment.

Materials

- Fiddle tunes: "I'se the B'y," "Road to Boston," "Old Joe Clark," or any other eight-to-sixteen-bar fiddle tune

Prior Knowledge and Experiences

- Students have experience playing traditional fiddle tunes by rote.
- Students have experience improvising simple variations on a melody.
- Students have experience determining chord roots to simple folk songs.

Procedures

1. Teach the class a traditional fiddle tune by rote, dividing the melody into small sections as appropriate for the ability of the group. Guide the students in using characteristic bowings and expression.

2. Demonstrate rhythmic variations such as shuffle bowing (an eighth note followed by two sixteenths, played in a syncopated style, accenting the first sixteenth note). Explore with students simple melodic variations (such as double stops and addition or deletion of melody notes).

3. Ask students to determine the harmonic structure by playing the roots of the I, IV, and V chords, as appropriate, creating a bass line while you play the melody. (For detailed steps, see Strategy 3A in Grades 5–8 section.) Subsequently, have students add other chord tones and a characteristic accompanying rhythm to the harmony parts.

4. When all students can play the melody and improvise the accompanying harmony, assign students to play each part.

5. Have students play their assigned parts, and encourage them to improvise on their parts according to their ability.

Indicators of Success

- Students improvise rhythmic and melodic variations using characteristic bowings and style.
- Students determine a bass line and improvise harmony parts.
- The class performs the entire fiddle tune and accompaniment.

Follow-up

- Have students use the same procedures to improvise variations on other traditional fiddle tunes. Create a medley of the tunes.
- Ask individual students to improvise rhythmic and melodic variations while other students play the melody or the harmony straight.
- Select students to play an accompaniment on a guitar or a chorded zither (such as Autoharp or ChromAharp).

STANDARD 3E

Improvising melodies, variations, and accompaniments: *Students improvise original melodies in a variety of styles, over given chord progressions, each in a consistent style, meter, and tonality.*

Objective

- Students will improvise a melody over a designated chord progression in a consistent style, meter, and tonality

Materials

- Recording of "Tears of Joy," from *Ariel,* performed by Jerry Goodman, Private Music 2013
- Audio-playback equipment
- Rhythmic background from a commercially available recording, a MIDI setup, or a portable keyboard
- Chord progression from "Tears of Joy," notated on chalkboard

Prior Knowledge and Experiences

- Students have a thorough understanding of scales and arpeggios in major and minor keys and can perform them with facility.
- Students can follow a notated chord progression.
- Students can determine the meter of odd-metered compositions.

Procedures

1. Play the recording of "Tears of Joy." Ask students to determine the meter (13/16) and tonality (E minor) by plucking the open strings of their instruments as the recording is being played.

2. Once the tonality has been established, ask the class to play the scale that corresponds to the E minor tonality. Enhance their playing of the scale by providing a rhythmic accompaniment from an audio recording, a MIDI setup, or a portable keyboard.

3. Once the students can perform the scale accurately, choose one student at a time to improvise a melody in the key of E minor. (The melody should start very simply with the first student and progress into a fully developed phrase as each of four or five volunteers performs his or her improvisation.)

4. Ask the class to perform the chord progression from "Tears of Joy" that is notated on the chalkboard. Have the class perform the chord progression without a soloist.

5. Select a student to start improvising a melody on the progression using the meter and rhythmic style of "Tears of Joy." Repeat this until each student has had an opportunity to be the soloist.

Indicators of Success

- Students improvise a melody over a given chord progression in the style, meter, and tonality of "Tears of Joy."

Follow-up

- Have students improvise melodies using the same procedures with a composition in a different key.
- Have students follow the same procedures, in a different style, such as rock and roll or waltz.
- Using a rhythm section of piano, bass, and drums, have students improvise on the melody of a jazz standard (such as "Five Foot Two" or "On the Sunny Side of the Street") or a show tune (such as "Send in the Clowns" or "Try to Remember").

STANDARD 3E

Improvising melodies, variations, and accompaniments: Students improvise original melodies in a variety of styles, over given chord progressions, each in a consistent style, meter, and tonality.

Objective

- Students will improvise melodies and melodic fragments over a harmonic accompaniment in a consistent style, meter, and tonality.

Materials

- Chord progression for harmonization of a familiar tune on handouts or chalkboard

- Keyboard (or recording with chord progression from the familiar tune)

- Audio-playback equipment, if recording is used

Prior Knowledge and Experiences

- Students know the difference, aurally and theoretically, between major and minor tonality and can perform corresponding major and minor scales. They can imitate short melodic patterns in these keys.

- Students have some experience playing triads on a given pitch.

Procedures

1. Review several major and minor scales and have students imitate short melodic patterns with a variety of articulations, including those in jazz and swing styles, using teacher demonstration–student imitation method.

2. Using one scale, ask the class to play a triad (arpeggio) on each scale degree.

3. As you play the chord progression (shown on handouts or on the chalkboard) on the keyboard or from a recording, have students improvise melodic patterns over this chord progression. Explain that melodic patterns can be developed in a variety of ways (for example, by changing the order of chord tones or by changing rhythm patterns).

Indicators of Success

- Students improvise melodies over a given harmonic accompaniment.

Follow-up

- Have students expand their improvisation skills by improvising in the blues style. Ask the class to play a triad (arpeggio) on each scale degree of a blues scale. Write a twelve-bar blues progression on the chalkboard or on a handout. Play recordings of blues performances. Using a recording of harmonic and melodic backgrounds (such as "Slow Blues" in F and A, from *Nothin' but Blues,* vol. 2 of Jamey Aebersold's *A New Approach to Jazz Improvisation,* Jamey Aebersold Jazz 1971, side 1, track 3), have some students improvise melodic patterns based on the blues progression and then improvise rhythmic variations. Limit the length of the patterns to four measures at first. Have students expand the length of their melodic patterns to eight measures and then twelve measures.

STANDARD 5B

Reading and notating music: Students sightread, accurately and expressively, music with a level of difficulty of 3, on a scale of 1 to 6.

Objective

■ Students will sightread an instrumental work with a level of difficulty of 3.

Materials

■ Brandenburg Concerto no. 5 by J. S. Bach, arr. Merle J. Isaac, (Van Nuys, CA: Highland-Etling/Alfred Publishing Company, 1990), Level 3

■ Chalkboard

Prior Knowledge and Experiences

■ Students have performed music with a level of difficulty of 4.

■ Students can maintain a consistent tempo while sightreading.

■ Students can predict potential problem spots, such as key changes and tempo changes, by looking at their parts.

Procedures

1. Ask students to study their parts silently, noting any problem spots.

2. Conduct and sing through the Brandenburg Concerto no. 5 on a neutral syllable or with counting syllables. Ask students to shadow bow (follow their parts and move their bows silently in the air) while you sing. During this run-through, use voice inflection and appropriate conducting gestures to indicate tempo changes, expressive features of the piece, and which section of the orchestra has the part you are singing.

3. At the end of the shadow bowing exercise, invite questions students may have (for example, a question about a specific rhythm, bow placement, a type of bow stroke, or possible fingering problems).

4. Have students identify sections of the piece that are similar to the beginning of the piece.

5. Conduct the students in playing the piece without any verbal direction.

Indicators of Success

■ Students play through the piece without stopping and with an 80 percent accuracy rate for notes and rhythms.

Follow-up

■ Have students play through the same piece pizzicato, focusing on pitch accuracy. To improve accuracy, ask one section of the orchestra to play arco in a selected passage while the rest of the orchestra shadow bows.

■ Have students listen to an excellent recording of the same piece. Ask them to finger and shadow bow their parts. Then have them play the piece.

STANDARD 6C

Listening to, analyzing, and describing music: Students identify and explain compositional devices and techniques used to provide unity and variety and tension and release in a musical work and give examples of other works that make similar uses of these devices and techniques.

Objective

■ As students perform and listen to a fugue, they will identify, aurally and visually, successive entrances of the subject.

Materials

■ "Prelude and Fugue in D Major," from *Eight Little Preludes and Fugues* by J. S. Bach, arr. Robert S. Frost (Grand Rapids, MI: Lake State Publishers, 1985), Level 5

■ Chart (on chalkboard) for recording information about subject entrances in the fugue (see accompanying figure)

Prior Knowledge and Experiences

■ Students can play an arrangement of Bach's "Prelude and Fugue in D Major."

■ Students can recognize statements of the fugue theme (subject) at different pitch levels, played by different instruments.

Procedures

1. Lead the orchestra in playing the exposition of the fugue from Bach's "Prelude and Fugue in D Major."

2. Have students play the exposition, stopping at the entrance of each statement of the fugue subject. Identify which instrument(s) plays each statement of the subject. After the students have played each segment, ask a student volunteer to record on the chart (drawn on the chalkboard) the measure numbers of each segment and which instrument has the subject.

3. Have students examine and discuss the results. (For example, "How many statements are there?" "Does each statement begin on the same pitch?") Have the student volunteer record on the chart the scale degree on which each statement begins.

4. Discuss the intervallic or key relationships of the various statements of the subject. (For example, "At what intervals do the second and third statements begin?" "Does the tonality remain the same or does it change?") Have the student volunteer record on the chart the key for each statement of the subject.

5. Lead the orchestra in performing the exposition of the fugue again, asking students to give particular attention to each entrance of the subject.

Indicators of Success

■ Students identify the initial group of entrances as the exposition.

■ Students aurally and visually identify successive entries of the subject as they perform and listen to the exposition of a fugue.

(continued)

Follow-up

- Have students play the entire fugue, continuing to identify statements of the subject material. Have students determine whether each entrance is a complete statement of the subject and whether the entrances follow the same intervallic pattern as in the exposition.

- Develop a chart for the rest of the fugue. Discuss inversion, augmentation, and stretto.

- Encourage piano students, or others who have studied fugues, to play for the class.

Where (measure #s)	Who has the subject? (instrument part)	In what key? (e.g., D major)	Beginning on which scale degree? (e.g., fifth)
____ → ____			
____ → ____			
____ → ____			
____ → ____			

Subject entrances in exposition of fugue from Bach's "Prelude and Fugue in D Major."

STANDARD 6C

Listening to, analyzing, and describing music: *Students identify and explain compositional devices and techniques used to provide unity and variety and tension and release in a musical work and give examples of other works that make similar uses of these devices and techniques.*

Objective

- Students will identify, aurally and visually, the sections of sonata-allegro form and label each section correctly.

Materials

- Symphony no. 5 by Ludwig van Beethoven
- Recording of Beethoven's Symphony no. 5
- Audio-playback equipment
- Chalkboard

Prior Knowledge and Experiences

- Students have studied sonata-allegro form in preparing another piece, such as Serenade, K. 525, *Eine kleine Nachtmusik* by Wolfgang Amadeus Mozart.

Procedures

1. Review names of the sections of sonata-allegro form (exposition, development, recapitulation, coda), writing them on the chalkboard.

2. Distribute the parts to Beethoven's Symphony no. 5 and have students look over the first movement.

3. Ask students to label the sections of sonata-allegro form by visual analysis while you play a recording of the symphony's first movement. (*Note:* This step and those that follow can be modified by having students identify the theme groups within the exposition only; over the course of a number of lessons, the analysis can be extended to other sections of the movement.)

4. Replay the recording of the first movement. Indicate the arrival at each section by pointing to its name on the board. Have students check their labels for accuracy.

5. Rehearse the first movement, using only the section names, rather than rehearsal letters or measure numbers, as reference points.

Indicators of Success

- Students rehearse the first movement of the symphony successfully using section names as reference points rather than rehearsal letters or measure numbers.

Follow-up

- Use the same procedures with other music written in sonata-allegro form, such as the first movement of Mozart's Symphony no. 40.

- Extend the same procedure to the study of other formal structures, such as minuet-trio form, used in the third movement of Mozart's Symphony no. 40.

STANDARD 6E

Listening to, analyzing, and describing music: Students compare ways in which musical materials are used in a given example relative to ways in which they are used in other works of the same genre or style.

Objective

■ Students will identify, aurally and visually, compositional devices used by composers of the Baroque period and compare the ways they are used.

Materials

■ Concerto Grosso, op. 6, no. 8 ("Christmas") by Arcangelo Corelli (New York: Edwin F. Kalmus & Company, n.d.), Level 4

■ List of repertoire previously studied (on chalkboard)

Prior Knowledge and Experiences

■ Students have studied music of the Baroque period, such as George Frideric Handel's *Water Music* and *Music for the Royal Fireworks* and Johann Pachelbel's Canon in D.

Procedures

1. Lead the entire orchestra in performing the ripieno (tutti) passage at the beginning of the third movement of Corelli's Concerto Grosso, op. 6, no. 8.

2. Ask the concertino (soloist group) to perform their portion of the composition, having the class listen particularly to the cello part.

3. From the list of pieces (on the chalkboard) they have previously studied, ask students to select a piece that sounds similar. Then list on the chalkboard the musical characteristics that are common to the two pieces (for example, slower notes in the lower voices against faster notes in the violin part; imitation in the violin parts).

4. Discuss musical characteristics or compositional devices (listed on the chalkboard) that are common to this period and add the following if they are not already on the list: continuo, concertino and ripieno in the concerto grosso, and contrapuntal lines as opposed to a single melody supported by a harmonic structure.

Indicators of Success

■ Students identify, aurally and visually, stylistic components of Baroque music.

Follow-up

■ Students perform music of this period in an appropriate style.

■ Use a similar approach to analyze stylistic characteristics of the Classical period by having students study, perform, and identify common characteristics of two compositions, such as the minuet from Wolfgang Amadeus Mozart's *Eine kleine Nachtmusik* and the minuet from Joseph Haydn's Symphony no. 94 ("Surprise").

■ Have students read about Corelli's trio and solo sonatas, op. 1–6, in a general reference on the history of Western music, such as *A History of Western Music,* 4th ed., Donald J. Grout and Claude Palisca (New York: W. W. Norton & Company, 1988) and compare them to Corelli's Concerto Grosso, op. 6, no. 8, with regard to number, order, and tempo of movements, as well as to the list of characteristics developed by the class.

Proficient

STANDARD 7A

Evaluating music and music performances: Students evolve specific criteria for making informed, critical evaluations of the quality and effectiveness of performances, compositions, arrangements, and improvisations and apply the criteria in their personal participation in music.

Objective

■ Using criteria they have developed, students will critically evaluate their own performance and performances by others within their section and ensemble and apply the evaluations to improve such performances.

Materials

■ Any music the orchestra is learning

■ Audiotape of the orchestra

■ Audiocassette recorder

Prior Knowledge and Experiences

■ Students have developed criteria for evaluating technical as well as artistic aspects of performance.

■ Students have critiqued both their individual performances and those of their ensemble.

Procedures

1. Have students listen to a recording of their orchestra rehearsing a piece for performance.

2. Based on the criteria they have developed, ask students to write (using appropriate vocabulary) an evaluation of their performance, their section's performance, and the ensemble's performance. (Their critique should include evaluation of articulation, tone, dynamics, pitch, phrasing, and balance, as well as suggestions for improvement.)

3. After collecting all critique sheets, play the recording again and make appropriate and positive comments on the students' sheets. In reading the student sheets aloud, be sensitive to students' different levels of advancement. When appropriate, use a cooperative learning approach: Ask each section of the orchestra (violin I, violin II, viola, cello, bass) to work as a group, discussing the criteria and evaluating their own section. Have each section share its evaluation with the rest of the class.

Indicators of Success

■ Students use established criteria to evaluate the strengths and weaknesses of their individual performance, their section's performance, and the ensemble's performance.

■ Students provide insightful comments and suggest measures for improving their performances.

Follow-up

■ Have students evaluate their own solo performances.

■ Have students compare the criteria they developed to the adjudication form used at the state or regional level.

■ As students listen to other performances, have them write critiques. Keep critiques in their portfolios.

STANDARD 7B

Evaluating music and music performances: *Students evaluate a performance, composition, arrangement, or improvisation by comparing it to similar or exemplary models.*

Objective

- Students will evaluate classmates' performances by comparing them to a professional recording.

Materials

- Paper or index cards to be used for evaluations (separate paper or card for each student for writing about every other student in the class)

- Any piece in the students' folders that they have performed or are prepared to perform

Prior Knowledge and Experiences

- Students have learned to play the assigned piece of music.

- Students have developed a set of criteria by which the performance will be evaluated. (They may refer to an adjudication form used at the state or regional level.)

- Students have listened to and discussed a professional recording of the assigned piece.

Procedures

1. Review the terminology used in the students' evaluative criteria (such as intonation, articulation, or rhythm), verbally and with live demonstration, if necessary.

2. Discuss appropriate ways to give positive and constructive evaluative comments, highlighting the importance of giving specific suggestions (for example, stating specifically what was good about the performance, rather than saying simply "good").

3. Distribute the papers to be used for evaluations. Announce the name of the first performer and ask students to write that person's name on their papers. While each student performs, have others write one thing they think that person did well and one thing that could be improved, keeping in mind their evaluative criteria and previous discussion about the professional recording.

4. Continue the process until all students have performed. (The student who is performing may or may not choose to write comments after his or her performance.)

5. Collect all the comment sheets. (Before the next class, check the comments for appropriateness and usefulness; some papers may need to be omitted. Return every student's comments to each performer.)

Indicators of Success

- Students write specific and appropriate evaluative comments about their classmates' performances by comparing them to the performance on the professional recording.

Follow-up

- In preparing for a solo-ensemble festival, have students listen to a professional recording of the selections to be performed. As their peers perform, have students make written evaluations of the student performances, using the same criteria that will be used at the festival.

- In preparing for an orchestra festival, make an audio or video recording of the group and have students compare it to a professional recording. Students should write their comments using the same criteria that will be used at the festival.

Proficient

STANDARD 8A

Understanding relationships between music, the other arts, and disciplines outside the arts:
Students explain how elements, artistic processes, and organizational principles are used in similar and distinctive ways in the various arts and cite examples.

Objective

- Students will identify and explain how the theme of war is used in similar and distinctive ways in specific works in two art forms.

Materials

- Slide or print of Pablo Picasso's *Guernica*

- Slide projector, if slide is used

- Recording of "Threnody to the Victims of Hiroshima" by Krysztof Penderecki

- Audio-playback equipment

Prior Knowledge and Experiences

- Students can identify and describe the elements of music (rhythm, melody, harmony, and form).

- Students can identify and describe the organizational principles of music (tempo, repetition, contrast, dynamics, timbre, and tessitura).

Procedures

1. Have students view a reproduction of *Guernica*.

2. Have students listen to a recording of "Threnody to the Victims of Hiroshima."

3. Present and discuss the terms *avant garde, cubism,* and *sensualism*.

4. Present and discuss the elements of art (line, value, texture, color, shape, form, and space) and compare these to the elements of music (rhythm, melody, harmony, and form).

5. Present and discuss the organizational principles of art (repetition, unity, proportion, contrast, movement, balance, emphasis) and compare them to the organizational principles of music (tempo, repetition, contrast, dynamics, timbre, and tessitura).

6. Discuss and compare the artistic processes of the two artists (abstraction, dissonance, craftsmanship, imagination).

7. Discuss aesthetic judgments: good versus bad; pleasant versus unpleasant.

Indicators of Success

- Students verbalize successfully how the artistic processes, the elements of art and music, and the organizational principles of art and music are used to portray a theme of war in similar and distinctive ways in works by Picasso and by Penderecki.

Follow-up

- Have students bring in examples that reflect the theme of war or conflict from their popular culture (visual or musical). Discuss how the elements and organizational principles of those examples relate across arts disciplines.

- Have orchestra students rehearse "Morning," from Edvard Grieg's *Peer Gynt* and compare the feeling of morning with that evoked by Claude Monet's *Impression: Sunrise* or John Constable's *Hampstead Heath*.

- Discuss impressionism and follow steps 4–7 from the above procedures.

STANDARD 8B

Understanding relationships between music, the other arts, and disciplines outside the arts:
*Students compare characteristics of two or more arts within a particular historical
period or style and cite examples from various cultures.*

Objective

- Aurally and visually, students will identify and compare the use of ABA form in the Classical period in music, art, and architecture.

Materials

- Prints or slides of Raphael's *Sistine Madonna,* Jacques-Louis David's *Oath of Horatio-David,* and the U.S. Capitol Building

- Opaque projector and screen, if prints are used

- Slide projector, if slides are used

- "Minuet," from Symphony no. 25 by Wolfgang Amadeus Mozart, arr. Ralph Matesky (Van Nuys, CA: Highland-Etling/Alfred Publishing Company, 1988), Level 5

- Recording of the minuet from Symphony no. 100 ("The Military") by Joseph Haydn

- Audio-playback equipment

- Piano

Prior Knowledge and Experiences

- Students have been working on the Mozart minuet and are able to play the entire movement.

- Students can identify aurally ABA form in music.

Procedures

1. Rehearse "Minuet" from Mozart's Symphony no. 25.

2. Explain to students that (1) form is the organizational element in the arts through which the artist or composer presents material so that there is variety for interest and unity to avoid chaos; (2) Classical artists derived their inspiration from ancient Greece, based on truth and perfection; and (3) Classical artists believed that a perfect form could be used to present an infinite number of different compositions (for example, Haydn and Mozart composed all their symphonies using sonata-allegro form as a first movement and a minuet-trio as a third movement).

3. Play "Twinkle, Twinkle, Little Star" on your instrument or the piano for the class and ask students to identify the sections in "Twinkle" (‖: A :‖ B, A). Ask students how this simple ternary form relates to their Mozart minuet, which has the following form:

   A   B   [trio]   A

   ‖: a :‖: ba :‖: c :‖: dc :‖ a | ba

4. Explain that their Mozart minuet is in Classical compound ternary form, which is used in almost all minuets composed by Mozart and Haydn. Play a recording of the minuet from Haydn's Symphony no. 100.

5. Show a print or slide of the U.S. Capitol Building. Have students identify the form. (ABA with the dome as B.)

6. Show prints or slides of Raphael's *Sistine Madonna* and David's *Oath of Horatio.* Have students identify the ABA form of these works, noting that each picture has a central figure balanced by figures and similar backgrounds on either side.

Indicators of Success

- Students demonstrate an understanding of ternary form in art, music, and architecture by identifying and comparing aurally or visually obvious representations of ABA form in these artistic media.

Follow-up

- Rehearse and study the minuet from Haydn's Symphony no. 100.
- Relate ABA to sonata-allegro form.
- Expand the discussion of characteristics of the Classical period to include clarity of line, simplicity, balance, and use of reason or restraint in the work of the artist or the composer.

STANDARD 8C

Understanding relationships between music, the other arts, and disciplines outside the arts:
Students explain ways in which the principles and subject matter of various disciplines outside the arts are interrelated with those of music.

Objective

- Students will explain the relationship between the length of a vibrating column of air and its musical sound (pitch).

Materials

- Six soda straws per group: one for each of the five students in a group and one to use as an "original" straw with precut reed (see step 1)
- One pair of scissors per group
- One worksheet per group (see step 7)

Prior Knowledge and Experiences

- Students can hear and identify the relative sounds of *do re mi fa sol* and *do'.*

Procedures

(*Note:* Consider inviting the physics teacher to teach this lesson with you.)

1. Have each student cut a reed in his or her straw, copying the reed on the "original" straw.

   Have students practice producing a sound on their full-length straws.

2. Have students count off from 1 to 5. Have Student #1 fold his or her straw in half (excluding the reed), cut the straw in half at the fold, play the straw, and compare that pitch to the original pitch. (It will sound one octave higher, producing a high *do.*)

3. Have Student #2 cut Student #1's straw stub (the unused portion) in half, using it as a template to cut one-fourth of the straw off his or her original straw. Have Student #2 play his or her straw and compare it to the original pitch. (It will sound a perfect fourth higher—*fa.*)

4. Have Student #3 cut Student #2's straw stub in half, using it as a template to cut one-eighth of the straw off his or her original straw. Have the student play the straw and compare its pitch to the original pitch. (It will sound a major second higher—*re.*)

5. Have Student #4 fold a full-length straw in thirds and cut the lower third off at the fold. Have the student play the straw and compare the sound to the original pitch. (It will sound a perfect fifth higher—*sol.*)

6. Have Student #5 cut the stub from Student #4's straw in half and use it as a template to cut one-sixth of the straw off his or her straw. Have the student play the straw and compare its pitch to the original pitch. (It will sound a major third higher—*mi.*)

7. Have each group play their straws in order (original, 1, 2, 3, 4, 5), with Student #1 playing the original straw as well as his or her own. Have each group complete a chart, identifying the relationship of each straw length and resulting pitch (as in the following sample chart).

REMOVED	REMAINING	SOUND
none	all	*do*
1/2	1/2	*do'*
1/4	3/4	*fa*
1/8	7/8	*re*
1/3	2/3	*sol*
1/6	5/6	*mi*

Indicators of Success

- Students can explain the relationship between the length of the straw and the resulting pitches.

Follow-up

- Ask each group to arrange itself in order from 1 to 5 and play simple songs using the notes available.

- Have the groups perform for each other or all together.

- Have string students relate this project to the natural harmonics produced by a string when touched lightly at nodal points; have brass players relate this project to the overtone series on their instruments.

STANDARD 8D

Understanding relationships between music, the other arts, and disciplines outside the arts:
Students compare the uses of characteristic elements, artistic processes, and organizational principles among the arts in different historical periods and different cultures.

Objective

- As they perform characteristic pieces and view representative paintings, students will recognize, aurally and visually, and will describe the characteristic elements of music and art of the Classical and Romantic periods.

Materials

- *Romeo and Juliet* Introduction and Finale by Pyotr Il'yich Tchaikovsky, arr. J Frederick Müller (San Diego: Neil A. Kjos Music Company, 1964), Level 4

- First and fourth movements of Symphony no. 25 by Wolfgang Amadeus Mozart, arr. Ralph Matesky (Van Nuys, CA: Highland-Etling/Alfred Publishing Company, 1988), Level 5

- Slides or prints of *Liberty Leading the People* and *Abduction of Rebecca* by Eugène Delacroix, *Oath of Horatio* by Jacques-Louis David, and *Sistine Madonna* by Raphael

- Slide projector, if slides are used

- Opaque projector, if prints are used

Procedures

1. Rehearse the orchestra in the *Romeo and Juliet* Introduction and Finale.

2. Have students discuss the question, "How do the musical materials and organizational principles in this piece differ from those of minuets by Mozart and Haydn?"

3. If the discussion does not include it, be sure to point out the differences in orchestration, melodic line, form (story content), harmony, and emotional quality between the Tchaikovsky and Mozart music under study.

4. Show students the Delacroix paintings and discuss with them the differences between these and the paintings of David and Raphael. Point out the clarity of line in the Classical art, the motion in the Delacroix paintings, the emotional content in the Delacroix paintings, and the use of form by Delacroix as a means to an end, not an end in itself.

5. Continue rehearsing *Romeo and Juliet* Introduction and Finale. Explain the programmatic link to Shakespeare's *Romeo and Juliet*. Discuss the thematic material in the overture: Friar Laurence theme, the feud between the Montagues and the Capulets, Juliet's theme, and the transformation of Romeo's theme at the end.

6. Have students summarize the characteristic elements of these music and art works from the Classical and Romantic periods.

Indicators of Success

- Students recognize aurally and identify verbally characteristic elements of Classical and Romantic music and relate them to those in the visual arts.

Prior Knowledge and Experiences

- Students have rehearsed the minuet from Symphony no. 25.

- Students have discussed the characteristics of music of the Classical period, as well as ternary form.

- Students have listened to minuets by Mozart and Haydn.

- Students have had some experience rehearsing *Romeo and Juliet* Introduction and Finale.

Follow-up

- Rehearse "Great Gate of Kiev" by Modest Musorgsky and discuss its musical characteristics. Have students compare those characteristics to elements in the painting "The Great Gate of Kiev" by Victor Hartmann.

- After rehearsing Musorgsky's "Great Gate of Kiev" and discussing its musical characteristics, have students compare these characteristics to the music of Mozart and Tchaikovsky that they have studied.

STANDARD 9C

Understanding music in relation to history and culture: Students identify various roles that musicians perform, cite representative individuals who have functioned in each role, and describe their activities and achievements.

Objective

- Students will identify the roles of creative artists who have composed or arranged a piece and describe their work.

Materials

- Music reference materials (for example, *A History of Western Music,* 4th ed., Donald J. Grout and Claude Palisca (New York: W. W. Norton & Company, 1988); *The New Harvard Dictionary of Music,* Don Michael Randel, ed. (Cambridge, MA: Belknap Press of Harvard University Press, 1986); or *The Chronicle of Classical Music* by Alan Kendall (New York: Thames and Hudson, 1994)

Prior Knowledge and Experiences

- Students have been assigned to write short histories of the composers or arrangers whose music is presently being rehearsed, focusing on events in the composer's or arranger's life at the time the particular pieces were written. They have been asked to include information about the larger historical context of the time the piece was written, answering questions such as, "What was happening in the United States (or North America) at the time this piece was written or arranged?" "What was our town like at that time?" and "What was life like for people at that time?"

Procedures

1. Ask a student or team of students to present the assigned report on a composer or an arranger to the class. Distribute copies of the report to the class.

2. Assist the student(s) presenting the report(s) in a brief question-and-answer period about the composer. Relate the discussion to the music they are studying.

3. Ask students to keep these reports in their folders so they may refer to them when rehearsing their music.

Indicators of Success

- Students participate in discussions about composers or arrangers of music they are studying.

Follow-up

- At subsequent rehearsals, have other students present their reports. Distribute copies to the class and have a brief discussion. Use and review this information during the course of rehearsing the piece, and present a short quiz on the material during a rehearsal.

- Lead brief discussions about the conductors and soloists who have performed the particular works.

- Prepare, or have students (or teams of students) prepare, a discography of the repertoire being studied. Copy and distribute to ensemble members.

RESOURCES

Orchestra Scores Referenced in This Text

"Air for Strings" by Norman Dello Joio. Miami: Belwin Mills/Warner Bros. Publications, 1967. Level 3.

"Andante Festivo" by Jean Sibelius. New York: Southern Music Company, 1941. Level 3.

Andante from Symphony no. 94 in G ("Surprise") by Joseph Haydn, arr. Sandra Dackow. Cleveland: Ludwig Music Publishing Company, 1989. Level 3.

Brandenburg Concerto no. 5 by J. S. Bach, arr. Merle J. Isaac. Van Nuys, CA: Highland-Etling/Alfred Publishing Company, 1990. Level 3.

"Classical Bash," in *Strictly Strings*, Book 2, by Jacquelyn Dillon, James Kjelland, and John O'Reilly. Van Nuys, CA: Alfred Publishing Company, 1993. Level 1.

"Classical Dance" by Ken Cooper. Phoenix, AZ: C. R. Reiter Publishing (1101 East Morrow Dr., Phoenix, AZ 85024-2930), 1992. Level 2.

Concerto Grosso, op. 6, no. 8 ("Christmas") by Arcangelo Corelli. New York: Edwin F. Kalmus & Company, n.d. Level 4.

"Fanfare for Strings" by Doris Gazda. San Diego: Neil A. Kjos Music Company, 1994. Level 2.

"Great Gate of Kiev" by Modest Musorgsky.

"Intrada," from *Suite for Strings* by Samuel Scheidt, arr. Robert Klotman. Van Nuys, CA: Alfred Publishing Company, 1982. Level 2.

"Jesu, Joy of Man's Desiring" by J. S. Bach, arr. Reginald Jacques. Carey, NC: Oxford University Press, 1949. Level 4.

Peer Gynt by Edvard Grieg.

"Prelude and Fugue in D Major," from *Eight Little Preludes and Fugues* by J. S. Bach, arr. Robert S. Frost. Grand Rapids, MI: Lake State Publishers, 1985. Level 5.

"Rhosymedre" by Ralph Vaughan Williams, arr. Arnold Foster. Boston: Galaxy Music Company, 1938; distributed by ECS Publishing. Level 4.

Romeo and Juliet Introduction and Finale by Pyotr Il'yich Tchaikovsky, arr. J. Frederick Müller. San Diego: Neil A. Kjos Music Company, 1964. Level 4.

Rosamunde Overture by Franz Schubert, arr. Vernon Leidig. Van Nuys, CA: Highland-Etling/Alfred Publishing Company, 1991. Level 3.

Serenade, K. 525, *Eine kleine Nachtmusik* by Wolfgang Amadeus Mozart.

Simple Symphony by Benjamin Britten. London: Oxford University Press, 1963. Level 5.

"Song of Jupiter" by George Frideric Handel, arr. Leroy Anderson. Boca Raton, FL: Edwin F. Kalmus & Company, 1952. Level 3.

Suite for Strings by Samuel Scheidt, arr. Robert Klotman. Van Nuys, CA: Alfred Publishing Company, 1982. Level 4.

Symphony no. 1, Fourth Movement, by Johannes Brahms, arr. Vernon Leidig. Van Nuys, CA: Highland-Etling/Alfred Publishing Company, 1990. Level 3.

Symphony no. 5 by Ludwig van Beethoven.

Symphony no. 25, Wolfgang Amadeus Mozart, arr. Ralph Matesky. Van Nuys, CA: Highland-Etling/Alfred Publishing Company, 1988. Level 5.

Symphony no. 40 by Wolfgang Amadeus Mozart.

"Themes from the Moldau" by Bedrich Smetana, arr. Robert S. Frost. Delevan, NY: Kendor Music, 1982. Level 3.

"Unfinished" Symphony by Franz Schubert.

Vocal Scores Referenced in This Text

"Where'er You Walk," from *Semele* by George Frideric Handel.

Listening Selections Referenced in This Text

Aebersold, Jamey. *Nothin' but Blues,* vol. 2 of *A New Approach to Jazz Improvisation.* Jamey Aebersold Jazz 1971.

Beethoven, Ludwig van. Symphony no. 5.

Goodman, Jerry. *Ariel.* Private Music 2013.

Haydn, Joseph. Symphony no. 94 ("Surprise").

————. Symphony no. 100 ("The Military").

King Sunnyadé and His African Beats. *Synchro System*. Mango/Island Records 162-539737.

Mahler, Gustav. Symphony no. 1.

Mozart, Wolfgang Amadeus. Serenade, K. 525, *Eine kleine Nachtmusik*.

————. Symphony no. 40.

Offenbach, Jacques. "Barcarolle."

Penderecki, Krysztof. "Threnody to the Victims of Hiroshima."

Vaughan Williams, Ralph. *English Folk Song Suite*. Cleveland Symphonic Winds. Frederick Fennell. Telarc compact disc 80099.

Village Music of Bulgaria. Produced by Ethel Rain and Martin Koenig. Elektra/Nonesuch compact disc 79195-2.

Books Referenced in This Text

Anderson, Gerald E., and Robert S. Frost. *All for Strings,* Book 1. San Diego, CA: Neil A. Kjos Music Company, 1982.

Baker, Theodore. *Baker's Biographical Dictionary of Musicians*. 8th ed., rev. Slonimsky, Nicholas. New York: G. Schirmer, 1992.

Fletcher, Stanley. *New Tunes for Strings,* Book 1. Instructional design by Paul Rolland. New York: Boosey & Hawkes, 1971.

Frost, Robert S. *Primo Performance*. San Diego: Neil A. Kjos Music Company, 1994.

Grout, Donald J., and Claude Palisca. *A History of Western Music*. 4th ed. New York: W. W. Norton & Company, 1988.

Herfurth, C. Paul. *Early Classics for Beginning String Quartet or String Orchestra*. Boston: Boston Music Company, 1965.

Hotchkiss, Gwen, ed. *Loyola University Music Education Leadership Symposia: Implications of National Music Standards for String Education*. Elkhardt, IN: United Musical Instruments, 1995.

Kendall, Alan. *The Chronicle of Classical Music*. New York, Thames and Hudson, 1994.

Leonhard, Charles, *Status of Arts Education in American Public Schools*. Urbana, IL: National Arts Education Research Center, University of Illinois at Urbana–Champaign, 1991.

Machlis, Joseph, ed. *Introduction to Contemporary Music,* 2d ed. New York: W. W. Norton & Company, 1979.

Randel, Don Michael, ed. *The New Harvard Dictionary of Music.* Cambridge, MA: Belknap Press of Harvard University Press, 1986.

Sadie, Stanley, ed. *The New Grove Dictionary of Music and Musicians.* London: Macmillan Publishers, 1980.

Suzuki, Shinichi. *Suzuki Violin School,* vol. 1. Secaucus, NJ: Summy-Birchard, 1978.

Additional Resources

Anderson, Gerald E. *Essentials for Strings.* San Diego: Neil A. Kjos Music Company, 1985.

Applebaum, Samuel. *String Builder.* Miami: CPP/Belwin/Warner Bros. Publications, 1960.

Barrett, Henry. *The Viola: Complete Guide for Teachers and Students.* Tuscaloosa, AL: University of Alabama Press, 1978.

*Boardman, Eunice, ed. *Dimensions of Musical Thinking.* Reston, VA: Music Educators National Conference, 1989.

Dillon, Jacquelyn A., and Casimer Kriechbaum. *How to Design and Teach a Successful School String and Orchestra Program.* San Diego: Neil A. Kjos Music Company, 1978.

Edwards, Arthur C. *Beginning String Class Method.* Dubuque, IA: William C. Brown, 1985.

Etling, Forest R. *Etling String Class Method.* 2 vols. Van Nuys, CA: Highland-Etling/Alfred Publishing Company, 1971–76.

Evans, Peter. *The Music of Benjamin Britten.* Minneapolis: University of Minnesota Press, 1979.

Galamian, Ivan. *Principles of Violin Playing and Teaching.* Englewood Cliffs, NJ: Prentice Hall, 1985.

Gigante, Charles. *Manual of Orchestral Bowings.* Bryn Mawr, PA: Theodore Presser Company, 1986.

Gillespie, Robert, Pamela Tellejohn Hayes, and Michael Allen. *Essential Elements for Strings.* Milwaukee: Hal Leonard Corporation, 1995.

Green, Barry. *The Fundamentals of Double Bass Playing.* Cincinnati, OH: Piper Press, 1971.

Green, Barry, and W. Timothy Gallwey. *The Inner Game of Music.* New York: Doubleday & Company, 1986.

Green, Elizabeth. *Guide to Orchestral Bowings.* American String Teachers Association, 1987.

———. *Orchestral Bowings and Routines.* American String Teachers Association, 1990.

———. *Teaching String Instruments in Classes.* American String Teachers Association, 1987.

Herrmann, Evelyn. *Shinichi Suzuki, The Man and His Philosophy.* Athens, OH: Ability Development, 1981.

Hunsberger, Donald, and Roy Ernst. *The Art of Conducting.* New York: Alfred A. Knopf, 1983.

Isaac, Merle J. *Merle Isaac String Method.* Chicago: M. M. Cole, 1966.

Jackson, Barbara, Joel Berman, and Kenneth Sarch. *The ASTA Dictionary of Bowing Terms for String Instruments.* American String Teachers Association, 1987.

Johnson, Sheila. *Young Strings in Action.* New York: Boosey & Hawkes, 1971.

Klotman, Robert. *Teaching Strings.* New York: Schirmer Books, 1988.

Lamb, Norman. *Guide to Teaching Strings.* 4th ed. Dubuque, IA: William C. Brown, 1984.

Matesky, Ralph. *Learn to Play a Stringed Instrument.* Van Nuys, CA: Alfred Publishing Company, 1970.

———. *Playing and Teaching Stringed Instruments.* 2 volumes. Englewood Cliffs, NJ: Prentice Hall, 1963.

———. *The Well Tempered String Player.* Van Nuys, CA: Alfred Publishing Company, 1978.

Müller, J. Frederick, and Harold W. Rusch. *Müller-Rusch String Method.* Book 1. San Diego: Neil A. Kjos Music Company, 1961.

Mullins, Shirley. *Teaching Music: The Human Experience.* Willow Park, TX: Media Services, 1985.

*Music Educators National Conference. *The Complete String Guide.* Reston, VA: MENC, 1988.

*————. *Teaching Stringed Instruments: A Course of Study.* Reston, VA: MENC, 1991.

*————. *Teaching Wind and Percussion Instruments: A Course of Study.* Reston, VA: MENC, 1991.

Oddo, Vincent. *Playing and Teaching the Strings.* Belmont, CA: Wadsworth Publishing Company, 1979.

Rabin, Marvin and Priscilla Smith. *Guide to Orchestral Bowing through Musical Styles.* Madison, WI: University of Wisconsin Press, 1984. Videocassette.

Rolland, Paul, and Marla Mutschler. *The Teaching of Action in String Playing.* Champaign–Urbana, IL: Illinois String Research Associates, 1974.

Stycos, R. *School Orchestra Director's Guide.* Portland, ME: Weston Walch, 1982.

Suzuki, Shinichi. *Nurtured by Love: The Classic Approach to Talent Education.* Athens, OH: Accura Music, 1987.

————. *Suzuki Bass School.* 2 vols. Secaucus, NJ: Summy-Birchard, 1991–93.

————. *Suzuki Cello School.* 3 vols. Revised. Secaucus, NJ: Summy-Birchard, 1991–92.

————. *Suzuki Viola School.* 3 vols. Secaucus, NJ: Summy-Birchard, 1981–83.

————. *Suzuki Violin School.* 3 vols. Secaucus, NJ: Summy-Birchard, 1978.

Wisniewski, Thomas J., and John M. Higgins. *Learning Unlimited String Method.* Milwaukee: Hal Leonard Corporation, 1976.

Young, Phyllis. *Playing the String Game: Strategies for Teaching Cello and Strings.* Austin, TX: University of Texas Press, 1978.

*Available from MENC

MENC Resources on Music and Arts Education Standards

Implementing the Arts Education Standards. Set of five brochures: "What School Boards Can Do," "What School Administrators Can Do," " What State Education Agencies Can Do," "What Parents Can Do," "What the Arts Community Can Do." 1994. #4022. Each brochure is also available in packs of 20.

Music for a Sound Education: A Tool Kit for Implementing the Standards. 1994. #1600.

National Standards for Arts Education: What Every Young American Should Know and Be Able to Do in the Arts. 1994. #1605.

Opportunity-to-Learn Standards for Music Instruction: Grades PreK–12. 1994. #1619.

Performance Standards for Music: Strategies and Benchmarks for Assessing Progress Toward the National Standards, Grades PreK–12. 1996. #1633.

Perspectives on Implementation: Arts Education Standards for America's Students. 1994. #1622.

"Prekindergarten Music Education Standards." Brochure. 1995. #4015 (set of 10).

The School Music Program—A New Vision: The K–12 National Standards, PreK Standards, and What They Mean to Music Educators. 1994. #1618.

Summary Statement: Education Reform, Standards, and the Arts. 1994. #4001 (pack of 10); #4001A (single copy).

"Teacher Education for the Arts Disciplines: Issues Raised by the National Standards for Arts Education." 1996. #1609.

Teaching Examples: Ideas for Music Educators. 1994. #1620.

The Vision for Arts Education in the 21st Century. 1994. #1617.

MENC's *Strategies for Teaching* Series

Strategies for Teaching Prekindergarten Music, compiled and edited by Wendy L. Sims. #1644.

Strategies for Teaching K–4 General Music, compiled and edited by Sandra L. Stauffer and Jennifer Davidson. #1645.

Strategies for Teaching Middle-Level General Music, compiled and edited by June M. Hinckley and Suzanne M. Shull. #1646.

Strategies for Teaching High School General Music, compiled and edited by Keith P. Thompson and Gloria J. Kiester. #1647.

Strategies for Teaching Elementary and Middle-Level Chorus, compiled and edited by Ann Roberts Small and Judy Bowers. #1648.

Strategies for Teaching High School Chorus, compiled and edited by Randal Swiggum. #1649.

Strategies for Teaching Strings and Orchestra, compiled and edited by Dorothy A. Straub, Louis Bergonzi, and Anne C. Witt. #1652.

Strategies for Teaching Middle-Level and High School Keyboard, compiled and edited by Martha F. Hilley and Tommie Pardue. #1655.

Strategies for Teaching Beginning and Intermediate Band, compiled and edited by Edward J. Kvet and Janet M. Tweed. #1650.

Strategies for Teaching High School Band, compiled and edited by Edward J. Kvet and John E. Williamson. #1651.

Strategies for Teaching Specialized Ensembles, compiled and edited by Robert A. Cutietta. #1653.

Strategies for Teaching Middle-Level and High School Guitar, compiled and edited by William E. Purse, James L. Jordan, and Nancy Marsters. #1654.

Strategies for Teaching: Guide for Music Methods Classes, compiled and edited by Louis O. Hall with Nancy R. Boone, George N. Heller, and Rosemary C. Watkins. #1656.

For more information on these and other MENC publications, write to or call MENC Publications Sales, 1806 Robert Fulton Drive, Reston, VA 20191-4348; 800-828-0229.